Cross-platform Desktop Application Development: Electron, Node, NW.js, and React

Build desktop applications with web technologies

Dmitry Sheiko

BIRMINGHAM - MUMBAI

Cross-platform Desktop Application Development: Electron, Node, NW.js, and React

Copyright © 2017 Packt Publishing

First published: July 2017

Production reference: 1260717

Published by Packt Publishing Ltd.
Livery Place
35 Livery Street
Birmingham
B3 2PB, UK.
ISBN 978-1-78829-569-7

www.packtpub.com

Credits

Author
Dmitry Sheiko

Reviewer
Dobrin Ganev

Commissioning Editor
Smeet Thakkar

Acquisition Editor
Shweta Pant

Content Development Editor
Roshan Kumar

Technical Editor
Akhil Nair

Copy Editors
Dhanya Baburaj
Shaila Kusanale
Akshata Lobo

Project Coordinator
Devanshi Doshi

Proofreader
Safis Editing

Indexer
Mariammal Chettiyar

Graphics
Jason Monteiro

Production Coordinator
Shraddha Falebhai

About the Author

Dmitry Sheiko is a web developer, blogger, and open source contributor, living and working in the lovely city of Frankfurt am Main, Germany.

Dmitry got hooked on computer programming in late 80s. Since 1998, he has been in web-development. Over the last few years, Dmitry has been creating desktop applications with NW.js/Electron. The very first solutions were made with JavaScript/Backbone, but then he switched to TypeScript/React/Redux.

Dmitry has authored dozens of projects at GitHub, including: nw-autoupdater, Pragmatic CSS, and a CommonJS compiler.

First, I would like to thank my family for their continuous support and for allowing me to realize my own potential. A special thanks to my father who first took me to an industrial computer center when I was about 3 years old. In a decade, with the advance of PCs, I realized that computers mean games and after a while, became curious enough about how the games were built to start learning programming.

Thanks to Crytek for giving me the opportunity to pursue my passion for research and development.

About the Reviewer

Dobrin Ganev is a Calgary-based software developer with years of experience in various domains, from large-scale distributed applications to frontend web development with the latest JavaScript frameworks. In recent years, he has been focusing on architecting and prototyping solutions in various subjects, such as enterprise search, GIS, predictive analytics, and real-time distributed systems.

www.PacktPub.com

For support files and downloads related to your book, please visit www.PacktPub.com.

Did you know that Packt offers eBook versions of every book published, with PDF and ePub files available? You can upgrade to the eBook version at www.PacktPub.com and as a print book customer, you are entitled to a discount on the eBook copy. Get in touch with us at service@packtpub.com for more details.

At www.PacktPub.com, you can also read a collection of free technical articles, sign up for a range of free newsletters and receive exclusive discounts and offers on Packt books and eBooks.

https://www.packtpub.com/mapt

Get the most in-demand software skills with Mapt. Mapt gives you full access to all Packt books and video courses, as well as industry-leading tools to help you plan your personal development and advance your career.

Why subscribe?

- Fully searchable across every book published by Packt
- Copy and paste, print, and bookmark content
- On demand and accessible via a web browser

Customer Feedback

Thanks for purchasing this Packt book. At Packt, quality is at the heart of our editorial process. To help us improve, please leave us an honest review on this book's Amazon page at `https://www.amazon.com/dp/1788295692`.

If you'd like to join our team of regular reviewers, you can e-mail us at `customerreviews@packtpub.com`. We award our regular reviewers with free eBooks and videos in exchange for their valuable feedback. Help us be relentless in improving our products!

*This book is gratefully dedicated to my beloved wife Olga and son Jan.
My dears, you were both so supportive and patient throughout my time of writing.
You helped me bring this book to life..*

Table of Contents

Preface

HTML5 desktop application development is gaining momentum, and it s no wonder if you take into consideration that JavaScript is now the most popular programming language on the web. The set of HTML5 features combined with Node.js and the runtime API is impressively rich, to say nothing of the countless Node.js modules available on GitHub. In addition, HTML5 desktop applications can be distributed across different platforms (Window, macOS, and Linux) without any modifications in the code.

The goal of this book is to help the reader discover what exciting opportunities unlock Node.js-driven runtime (NW.js and Electron) to a JavaScript developer and how surprisingly easy it is to catch up on programming specifics in this area.

What this book covers

Chapter 1, *Creating a File Explorer with NW.js - Planning, Designing, and Development*, shows that development starts with the blueprint of the file explorer application. We set up a development environment for NW.js and get a crash course on npm, which we will use to install any additional software, and build and run applications. We develop a static prototype of the application. On the way, we learn the best practices for writing maintainable CSS and get a brief introduction to ES2015.

Chapter 2, *Creating a File Explorer with NW.js - Enhancement and Delivery*, covers the extension and finalization of the application. For that, we master desktop environment integration APIs such as the clipboard, context menu, and tray. We provide file explorer with support for multiple languages and locales. We make it respond to command-line options. We examine pre-production aspects such as code protection, packaging, and autoupdate.

Chapter 3, *Creating a Chat System with Electron and React - Planning, Designing, and Development*, teaches us how to develop a chat system with Electron and React so, we get an introduction to both of them. We configure the Webpack bundler to transpile React components with JSX syntax. In addition, we make it process CSS files requested as modules. Thus, we can load the assets of the Electron-dedicated library Photonkit. We add the DevTool React extension in Electron and come up with a static prototype at the end of the chapter.

Chapter 4, *Creating a Chat System with Electron and React - Enhancement, Testing, and Delivery*, covers bringing the application to life. We use the Electron API and React state to implement windowing functions. We learn to use the WebSocket API to provide the chat with bidirectional communication. We examine the unit testing of views and services, and explore Electron-specific packaging, distribution, and autoupdates.

Chapter 5, *Creating a Screen Capturer with NW.js, React, and Redux - Planning, Design, and Development*, explains how to build a screen capturer based on global application state driven by Redux. In development, we use ready-made React components from the Material UI library. At the end of the chapter, we have a static prototype.

Chapter 6, *Creating a Screen Capturer with NW.js - Enhancement, Tooling, and Testing*, outlines how to make the application take screenshots and record screencasts. We learn to use WebRTC APIs to get the video stream. We make it generate a still frame image for screenshots and capture the video stream in a file for screencasts. We use the Notification API to inform the user about actions performed, regardless of what window is in focus. We make capturing actions available via global keyboard shortcuts.

Chapter 7, *Creating RSS Aggregator with Electron, TypeScript , React, and Redux - Planning, Design, and Development*, prepares us to develop a RSS aggregator. For that application, we take advantage of static typing with TypeScript and so, learn the essentials of programming languages. We build a static prototype with the React components of the React MDL library.

Chapter 8, *Creating RSS Aggregator with Electron, TypeScript, React, and Redux - Development*, explores how to develop the application. On the way, we will learn to use asynchronous actions, and access the store from React components and from services. We will also examine the peculiarities of rendering guest content in Electron.

What you need for this book

To build and run the examples in this book, you need either Linux or macOS; you will also need npm/Node.js. At the time of writing, the author tested the examples with the following software:

- npm v.5.2.0
- node v.8.1.1
- Ubuntu 16.04 LTS, Windows 10, and macOS Sierra 10.12

Who this book is for

This book has been written for any developers interested in creating desktop applications with HTML5. The first two chapters require essential web-master skills (HTML, CSS, and JavaScript) and the basics of Node.js. This part of the book includes a crash course on npm, which will be used across the book to build and run examples, given that you have experience with the command line in your OS (Linux, macOS, or Windows). The next four chapters welcome a minimal experience with React. And finally, for the last two chapters, it would be helpful to have a basic knowledge of TypeScript.

Conventions

In this book, you will find a number of text styles that distinguish between different kinds of information. Here are some examples of these styles and an explanation of their meaning.

Code words in text, database table names, folder names, filenames, file extensions, pathnames, dummy URLs, user input, and Twitter handles are shown as follows: "Well, we can change the locale and trigger the event. What about consuming modules?
In the `FileList` view, we have the `formatTime` static method that formats the passed-in `timeString` for printing. We can make format it in accordance with the currently chosen `locale`."

A block of code is set as follows:

```
{
  "name": "file-explorer",
  "version": "1.0.0",
  "description": "",
  "main": "main.js",
  "scripts": {
  "test": "echo "Error: no test specified" && exit 1"
  },
  "keywords": [],
  "author": "",
  "license": "ISC"
}
```

Any command-line input or output is written as follows:

```
sudo npm install nw --global
```

New terms and important words are shown in bold. Words that you see on the screen, for example, in menus or dialog boxes, appear in the text like this: "The menu **Show Item** contains **Folder**, **Copy**, **Paste**, and **Delete**."

Warnings or important notes appear in a box like this.

 Tips and tricks appear like this.

Reader feedback

Feedback from our readers is always welcome. Let us know what you think about this book--what you liked or disliked. Reader feedback is important for us as it helps us develop titles that you will really get the most out of.

To send us general feedback, simply e-mail feedback@packtpub.com, and mention the book's title in the subject of your message.

If there is a topic that you have expertise in and you are interested in either writing or contributing to a book, see our author guide at www.packtpub.com/authors.

Customer support

Now that you are the proud owner of a Packt book, we have a number of things to help you to get the most from your purchase.

Downloading the example code

You can download the example code files for this book from your account at http://www.packtpub.com. If you purchased this book elsewhere, you can visit http://www.packtpub.com/support and register to have the files e-mailed directly to you. You can download the code files by following these steps:

1. Log in or register to our website using your e-mail address and password.
2. Hover the mouse pointer on the **SUPPORT** tab at the top.
3. Click on **Code Downloads & Errata**.
4. Enter the name of the book in the **Search** box.
5. Select the book for which you're looking to download the code files.

6. Choose from the drop-down menu where you purchased this book from.
7. Click on **Code Download**.

Once the file is downloaded, please make sure that you unzip or extract the folder using the latest version of:

- WinRAR / 7-Zip for Windows
- Zipeg / iZip / UnRarX for Mac
- 7-Zip / PeaZip for Linux

The code bundle for the book is also hosted on GitHub at `https://github.com/PacktPubl ishing/Cross-platform-Desktop-Application-Development-Electron-Node-NW.js-an d-React`. We also have other code bundles from our rich catalog of books and videos available at `https://github.com/PacktPublishing/`. Check them out!

Downloading the color images of this book

We also provide you with a PDF file that has color images of the screenshots/diagrams used in this book. The color images will help you better understand the changes in the output. You can download this file from `https://www.packtpub.com/sites/default/files/down loads/CrossplatformDesktopApplicationDevelopmentElectronNodeNWJSandReact_Col orImages.pdf`.

Errata

Although we have taken every care to ensure the accuracy of our content, mistakes do happen. If you find a mistake in one of our books—maybe a mistake in the text or the code—we would be grateful if you could report this to us. By doing so, you can save other readers from frustration and help us improve subsequent versions of this book. If you find any errata, please report them by visiting `http://www.packtpub.com/submit-errata`, selecting your book, clicking on the Errata Submission Form link, and entering the details of your errata. Once your errata are verified, your submission will be accepted and the errata will be uploaded to our website or added to any list of existing errata under the Errata section of that title.

To view the previously submitted errata, go to `https://www.packtpub.com/books/conten t/support` and enter the name of the book in the search field. The required information will appear under the Errata section.

Piracy

Piracy of copyrighted material on the Internet is an ongoing problem across all media. At Packt, we take the protection of our copyright and licenses very seriously. If you come across any illegal copies of our works in any form on the Internet, please provide us with the location address or website name immediately so that we can pursue a remedy.

Please contact us at copyright@packtpub.com with a link to the suspected pirated material.

We appreciate your help in protecting our authors and our ability to bring you valuable content.

Questions

If you have a problem with any aspect of this book, you can contact us at questions@packtpub.com, and we will do our best to address the problem.

1
Creating a File Explorer with NW.js-Planning, Designing, and Development

Nowadays, when speaking of HTML5 desktop application development, one implies either **NW.js** or **Electron**. The first one has a shorter learning curve, which makes it a better choice for the beginning. Our first application will be a File Explorer. This sort of software is traditionally considered as a classical desktop application. I believe that you will find it exciting to build a File Explorer with HTML, CSS, and JavaScript. This chapter requires no skills in JavaScript frameworks, as we will use none. All you need is a basic knowledge of HTML, CSS, and plain JavaScript (including Node.js).

So, what are we up to? We will plan and sketch the project. We will set up the development environment and create a static prototype and run it with NW.js. We will implement the basic functionality, making it ready to be enhanced in `Chapter 2`, *Creating a File Explorer with NW.js–Enhancement and Delivery*.

The application blueprint

By File Explorer, I mean a small program that allows navigating through the filesystem and performs basic operations on the files, which can be expressed with the following user stories:

- As a user, I can see the content of the current directory
- As a user, I can navigate through the filesystem
- As a user, I can open a file in the default associated program

- As a user, I can delete a file
- As a user, I can copy a file in the clipboard and paste it later in a new location
- As a user, I can open the folder containing the file with the system file manager
- As a user, I can close the application window
- As a user, I can minimize the application window
- As a user, I can maximize and restore the application window
- As a user, I can change the application language

It would be easier to perceive it in a visual form, wouldn't it? Wireframes come in handy here. Wireframe is a skeletal framework of the application that depicts the arrangement of the application's content, including UI elements and navigation system. Wireframe has no real graphics, typography, or even colors. It shows schematically, what the application does. As you know, drawing with a pencil on a paper is possible, but it is not the best way to create a wireframe; what we need is a prototyping tool. Today, there are plenty of solutions on the market. Here, I use an impressive, but affordable tool called **WireframeSketcher** (`http://wireframesketcher.com/`). It allows you to sketch web, desktop, and mobile applications (just what we need). It also has a rich mock-up gallery of stencils, widgets, icons, and templates that makes prototyping fast and easy. Besides, the wireframes look nice in a sketchy style:

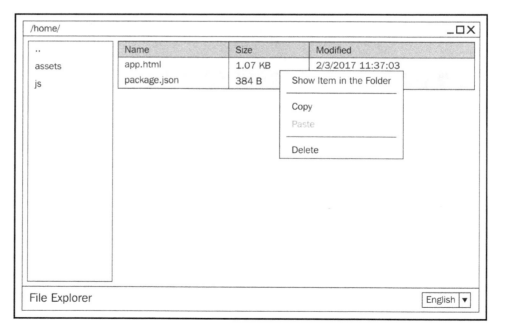

What we can see on the wireframe is often called a **Holy Grail Layout**. In our case, the header serves as the window title bar. There, we keep our controls for window actions such as close, maximize, and minimize. Besides that, in the title bar, we display the path to the current directory. In the sidebar, we have our filesystem navigation. The main section contains a table that represents files of the current directory. It has columns--**Name**, **Size**, and **Modified**. A right-click on a file opens a context menu with available file operations. The footer comprises the application title and a language selector combo box.

Setting up an NW.js project

NW.js is an open source framework for building HTML, CSS, and JavaScript applications. You can also see it as a headless browser (based on Chromium `https://www.chromium.org/`) that includes Node.js runtime and provides desktop environment integration API. Actually, the framework is very easy to start with. What we need is just a start page HTML file and project manifest file (`package.json`).

To see it in action, we will create a project folder named `file-explorer` at an arbitrary location. The choice of the folder location is up to you, but I personally prefer to keep web projects in `/<username>/Sites` on Linux/macOS and `%USERPROFILE%Sites` on Windows.

As we enter the directory, we create placeholder folders for JavaScript and CSS sources (`js` and `assets/css`):

```
[sheiko:file-explorer]$ tree .
.
├── assets
│   └── css
├── index.html
└── js
```

We also place a start page HTML (`index.html`) that consists of just a few lines:

```
./index.html
<!DOCTYPE html>
<html>
 <body>
  <h1>File Explorer</h1>
 </body>
</html>
```

As you can guess, we shall see just this text--**File Explorer**-- when feeding this file to a browser.

Now, we need the Node.js manifest file (`package.json`). Node.js, embedded in the framework, will use it to resolve dependency package names when called with a `require` function or from an npm script. In addition, NW.js takes from it the project configuration data.

Why not create the manifest file and populate it with dependencies using the npm tool?

Node Package Manager

Nowadays, **Node Package Manager (npm)** is one of the most demanded gadgets in the web developer tool belt. It's a command-line utility connected with the corresponding online repository of packages and is capable of package installation, version management, and dependency management. So, when we need a package (library, framework, and module), we will check whether it's available in the npm repository and run npm to bring it into our project. It not only downloads the package, it also resolves its dependencies and does it pretty smartly. Furthermore, npm is pretty handy as an automation tool. We can set various command-line tasks to refer any of the locally installed packages by name. The npm tool will find the executable package among installed packages and run it.

The npm tool is distributed together with Node.js. So, you can find an installer for Windows or for macOS on the Node.js download page (`https://nodejs.org/en/download`). It is also available as an APT package, so you can install it for Linux with the `apt-get` tools:

```
sudo apt-get install npm
```

If you have already installed npm, ensure that it's up to date:

```
sudo npm install npm@latest -g
```

As I have already said, we can install packages with npm-- for example, NW.js. If we want to do it globally, we will run the following command:

```
sudo npm install nw --global
```

Alternatively, we can run the following command:

```
sudo npm i nw -g
```

This will download the latest build of NW.js in `{prefix}/lib/node_modules/` and place the executable file in `{prefix}/bin`. It adds the binary to the `PATH` environment variable, so one can call `nw` in any location in the shell.

> `{prefix}` In order to find out what `{prefix}` is one can run:
> `npm config get prefix`. On Linux/macOS it will be `/usr/local`. On Windows `%APPDATA%npm`

This way, we will have a single instance of NW.js across the system, but what if an application requires a specific version of NW.js? Luckily, with npm, we can also install a package locally, and therefore, rely on a particular version that addresses our application. In addition, we can manage local dependencies in the `package.json` file. With a single command, npm can install/update all the dependencies enlisted there at once.

Let's take a look at how it works on our project. We go to the project root (the `file-explorer` folder) and run the following command:

```
npm init -y
```

It produces a `package.json` file with the following content:

```
{
  "name": "file-explorer",
  "version": "1.0.0",
  "description": "",
  "main": "main.js",
  "scripts": {
   "test": "echo "Error: no test specified" && exit 1"
  },
  "keywords": [],
  "author": "",
  "license": "ISC"
}
```

Here, in the `name` field, we set our application name. Beware that NW.js will use the provided value to name the directory in a system-dependent path for the project persistent data (`nw.App.dataPath`). So, it shall be a unique, lowercase alpha-numeric, but may include a few special symbols, such as `.`, `_`, and `-`.

Field version expects the application version as a string, conforming to the Semantic Versioning standard (`http://semver.org/`). What it all boils down to is a composite product version out of three numbers separated with dots. The first number (MAJOR) increments when we make incompatible API changes, the second number (MINOR) increases when we introduce a new functionality, and the last one (PATCH) identifies bug fixes.

In the `main` field, we let NW.js know where to find our start page HTML. We have to edit the manifest to change its value with `index.html`:

`./package.json`

```
{
   ...
   "main": "index.html",
   ...
}
```

The field `scripts` accepts a key value object with automation scripts for the project. By default, it has a placeholder for tests. Now, run the following command:

npm run test

The Shell responds with an error message saying **no test specified**, as we have no test yet. However, we will need a script to start the application. So, we edit `package.json` again and add to `scripts` field the following lines:

`package.json`

```
{
   ...
   "scripts": {
     "start": "nw .",
     "test": "echo "Error: no test specified" && exit 1"
   },

   ...
}
```

Now, we can type `npm run start` or `npm start` to run NW.js on the project root, but we do not have the framework installed, yet. We are just about to bring it in.

Manifest fields--such as description/keywords and author--help other people to discover the application as a package. The `license` field tells people how they are permitted to use the package. You can find more about these fields and other possible options at https://docs.npmjs.com/files/package.json.

Before telling npm to install the framework, we note that the standard version of NW.js doesn't include DevTools, which we definitely will need for development. So, we look for a specific version, the so-called SDK flavor. To find out the package versions that are available for the NW.JS package (`nw`), we run the following command:

```
npm view nw dist-tags
```

Alternatively, we can run the following command:

```
npm v nw dist-tags
```

This receives the following output:

```
{
  latest: '0.20.3',
  alphasdk: '0.13.0-alpha4sdk',
  alpha5sdk: '0.13.0-alpha5sdk',
  alpha6sdk: '0.13.0-alpha6sdk',
  alpha7sdk: '0.13.0-alpha7sdk',
  sdk: '0.20.3-sdk'
}
```

From this payload, we can assume that the latest version at the time of writing is 0.20.3 and that it is accompanied with 0.20.3-sdk. So, we can install the framework, as follows:

```
npm install nw@0.20.3-sdk --save-dev
```

Alternatively,we can install it, as follows:

```
npm i nw@0.20.3-sdk -D
```

Actually, since we know that the package has a dist-tag called `sdk`, we can also do it as follows:

```
npm i nw@sdk -D
```

Just after running any of these commands, we can find a new subdirectory named node_modules. There, npm installs local dependencies.

Have you noticed that we applied the `--save-dev` `(-D)` option? This way, we requested npm to save the package in our development dependency list. Observe that `package.json` is changed:

```
{
  "name": "file-explorer",
  "version": "1.0.0",
  "description": "",
  "main": "index.html",
  "scripts": {
    "start": "nw .",
    "test": "echo "Error: no test specified" && exit 1"
  },
  "keywords": [],
  "author": "",
  "license": "ISC",
  "devDependencies": {
    "nw": "^0.20.3-sdk"
  }
}
```

We installed the package as a development dependency because this SDK version is meant only for development. In `Chapter 2`, *Creating a File Explorer with NW.js–Enhancement and Delivery* we will examine the distribution and packaging techniques. So, you will see how we can bundle the application with a platform-specific NW.js production build.

Since we have reflected our dependency in the manifest file, we can update this and any further packages any time by running the following command:

npm update

If we lose `node_modules`(for example after cloning the project from remote GIT repository given the dependency folder is usually in the ignore list), we can install all the dependencies through the following command:

npm i

Have you noticed? In the `package.json`, we assigned `nw` package with version in, so called, caret range ^0.20.3-sdk. That means during the install/update process, npm will accept new versions with patch and minor updates, but no major versions.

The following are some useful npm commands:

npm i pkg-name: Installs the latest available version of a package

npm i pkg-name@version: Installs a concrete version of the package

npm i pkg-name -S: Installs package as a dependency and saves it in package.json

npm i pkg-name -D: Installs package as a development dependency and save in package.json

npm i: Installs all the dependencies (including development ones) enlisted in package.json

npm i --production: Installs dependencies but not development ones

npm list: Shows all the installed dependencies

npm uninstall nw --save: uninstalls a package and removes it from

npm un nw -S: shorter syntax package.json

At this point, we have the framework instance and package.json pointing to index.html. So, we can run the only script we have defined in the manifest file so far:

npm start

First, run it on NW.JS in Ubuntu:

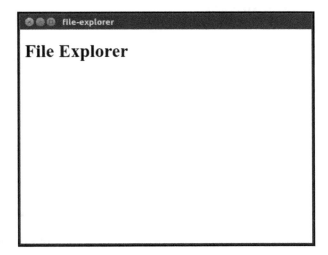

Then, run it on NW.JS in windows:

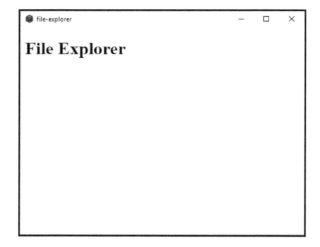

Finally, we run it in macOS:

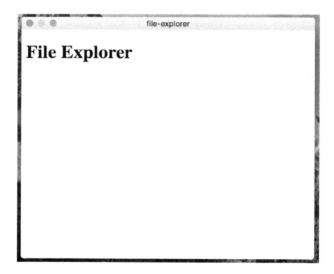

NW.js created a window and rendered index.html in it. It took the default Window parameters. If we want to customize them, we will need to edit package.json.

First, we will add the `window` field that accepts an object with the following properties:

- `window.icon`: This specifies a relative path to the window icon.
- `window.show`: This indicates whether the window is visible when the application starts or not. For instance, you can set it to false in the manifest and then change it programmatically with JavaScript (`nw.Window.get().show( true )`).
- `window.frame`: This makes the window frameless when set to `false`.
- `window.width` / `window.height`: This sets the window default size in pixels.
- `window.min_width` / `window.min_height`: This sets a minimal acceptable size to the window.
- `window.position`: This specifies where the window shall be placed. The value can be `null`, `center`, or `mouse`.
- `window.resizable`: When set to `true`, this property makes the window resizable.

We will also use the `chromium-args` field to specify the command-line arguments that we want to pass to chromium. Here, we set it to `--mixed-context` to switch NW.js into the corresponding mode. So, we could access the browser and the NW.js API directly from Node.js modules. NW.js introduces Node.js context in addition to the browser context and keep them separate. After extending it with NWJS meta-data the manifest looks as follows:
`./package.json`

```
{
  ...
  "chromium-args": "--mixed-context",
  "window": {
    "show": true,
    "frame": true,
    "width": 1000,
    "height": 600,
    "min_width": 800,
    "min_height": 400,
    "position": "center",
    "resizable": true
  }
}
```

These are just a few preferences set for our simple application. All the available options can be found at `https://github.com/nwjs/nw.js/wiki/manifest-format`.

An HTML prototype

We've just reached the point where we can start templating our application. Using HTML and CSS, we will achieve the intended look and feel. Later, we will bind JavaScript modules to the acting elements.

We start by replacing the content of `index.html` with the following code:

`./index.html`

```
<!DOCTYPE html>
<html>
  <head>
    <title>File Explorer</title>
    <meta charset="UTF-8">
    <meta name="viewport" content="width=device-width, initial-scale=1.0">
    <link href="./assets/css/app.css" rel="stylesheet" type="text/css">
  </head>
  <body class="l-app">
    <header class="l-app__titlebar titlebar">
    </header>
    <div class="l-app__main l-main">
    <aside class="l-main__dir-list dir-list">
    </aside>
    <main class="l-main__file-list file-list">
    </main>
    </div>
    <footer class="l-app_footer footer">
    </footer>
  </body>
</html>
```

Here, we just defined the page layout with semantically meaningful HTML tags. As you can see, we refer to `./assets/css/app.css` that we are about to create.

Maintainable CSS

Before we start styling, I would like to talk briefly about the importance of maintainability in CSS. Despite the fact that CSS is a declarative language, it requires no less diligence than any other code in general. When browsing a public repository, such as GitHub, you can still find plenty of projects where all the styles are put in a single file that is full of code smells (h ttps://csswizardry.com/2012/11/code-smells-in-css/) and has no consistency in class naming.

Well, it will not be much of a problem at the beginning, but CSS as any other code tends to grow. Eventually, you will end up with thousands of lines of rotting code often written by different people.

Then, you have to fix the UI element appearance, but you realize that dozens of existing CSS declarations across the cascade impact this element. You change one, and styles break unpredictably on other elements. So, you will likely decide to add your own rules overriding existing styles. After that, you may find out that some of the existing rules have a higher specificity, and you will have to use brute force through the cascade; every time it is going to be worse.

To avoid this maintainability problem, we have to break the entire application UI into components and design the CSS code so as to keep them reusable, portable, and conflict free; the following heuristics may come in handy:

- Split the whole CSS code into modules that represent components, layouts, and states
- Always use classes for styling (not IDs or attributes)
- Avoid qualified selectors (selectors with tags such as `nav`, `ul`, `li`, and `h2`)
- Avoid location dependency (long selectors such as `.foo`, `.bar`, `.baz`, and `article`)
- Keep selectors short
- Do not use `!important` reactively

There are different methodologies that help to improve CSS maintainability. Probably, the most popular approach is **Blocks Elements Modifiers** (**BEM**). It introduces a surprisingly simple, but powerful concept (`https://en.bem.info/methodology/key-concepts/`). It describes a pattern for class names that encourages readability and portability. I believe that the best way to explain it is by an example. Let's say we have a component representing a blog post:

```
<article class="post">
    <h2 class="post__title">Star Wars: The Last Jedi's red font is a
    cause for concern/h2>
    <time datetime="2017-01-23 06:00" class="post__time">Jan 23, 2017</time>
</article>
```

In BEM terminology, this markup represents a block that we can define with a class name `post`. The block has two elements--`post__title` and `post_time`. Elements are integral parts of a block; you cannot use them out of the parent block context.

Now imagine that we have to highlight one post of the list. So, we add a `post--sponsored` modifier to the block's classes:

```
<article class="post post--sponsored">
....
</article>
```

At first, class names containing double dashes and underscores may make you dizzy, but after a while you will get used to it. The BEM naming convention helps developers remarkably by showing indention. So when reading your own or somebody else's code, you can quickly figure out by its name what the purpose of a class is.

In addition to the BEM naming convention, we will use a few ideas from the Pragmatic CSS styleguide (`https://github.com/dsheiko/pcss`). We will give names prefixed with `is-` and `has-` to the classes representing global states (for example, `is-hidden` and `has-error`); we will prefix layout-related classes with `l-` (for example, `l-app`). Finally, we will amalgamate all CSS files in two folders (`Component` and `Base`).

Defining base rules

Firstly, we will create a `Base` directory and place the reset styles in there:

`./assets/css/Base/base.css`

```css
html {
  -webkit-font-smoothing: antialiased;
}

* {
  box-sizing: border-box;
}

nav > ul {
  list-style: none;
  padding: 0;
  margin: 0;
}

body {
  min-height: 100vh;
  margin: 0;
  font-family: Arial;
}

.is-hidden {
```

```
      display: none !important;
   }
```

For HTML scope, we will enable font smoothing for better font rendering.

Then, we will set box sizing of every element (*) in border-box. The default CSS box model is content-box, where width and height set to an element do not include padding and border. However, if we are setting, let's say, a sidebar width 250px, I would expect it to cover this length. With border-box, the box's size is always exactly what we set it, regardless of padding or border, but if you ask me, the border-box mode feels more natural.

We will reset indents and markers--for an unordered list--that are used for navigation (nav > ul). We make body element span the height of the entire viewport (min-height: 100vh), remove the default margin, and define the font family.

We will also introduce a global state is-hidden that can be applied on any element to remove it from the page flow. By the way, that is a good example of proactive and, therefore, permissible use of !important. By adding an is-hidden class (with JavaScript), we state that we want the element to hide, with no exceptions. Thus, we will never run into a specificity problem.

Defining layouts

That's enough for base styles; now, we will start on the layout. First, we will arrange the title bar, main section, and footer:

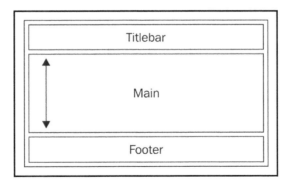

To achieve this design, we should preferably use Flexbox. If you are not familiar with this layout mode, I will recommend the article, *Understanding Flexbox: Everything you need to know* (http://bit.ly/2m3zmc1). It provides probably the most clear and easy-to-catch-up way of explaining what a Flexbox is, what options are available, and how to use them efficiently.

So, we can define the application layout like that:

./assets/css/Component/l-app.css

```css
.l-app {
  display: flex;
  flex-flow: column nowrap;
  align-items: stretch;
}

.l-app__titlebar {
  flex: 0 0 40px;
}

.l-app__main {
  flex: 1 1 auto;
}

.l-app__footer {
  flex: 0 0 40px;
}
```

We make .l-app a flex container that arranges inner items along a cross axis, vertically (flex-flow: column nowrap). In addition, we request the flex items to fill in the full height of the container (align-items: stretch). We set the title bar and footer to a fixed height always (flex: 0 0 40px). However, the main section may shrink and grow depending on the viewport size (flex: 1 1 auto).

Since we have an application layout, let's define the inner layout for the main section:

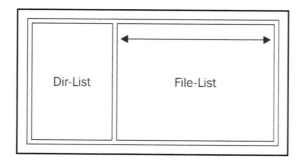

What we need to do is to make items--`dir-list` and `file-list`--to arrange horizontally one after another:

`./assets/css/Component/l-main.css`

```css
.l-main {
  display: flex;
  flex-flow: row nowrap;
  align-items: stretch;
}

.l-main__dir-list {
  flex: 0 0 250px;
}

.l-main__file-list {
  flex: 1 1 auto;
}
```

In the preceding code, we set the flex items to line up along an main axis horizontally using `flex-flow: row nowrap`. The `l-main__dir-list` item has a fixed width and its width depends on the viewport.

Actually, it's hard to see any results of our work until we give the components some colors:

`./assets/css/Component/titlebar.css`

```css
.titlebar {
  background-color: #2d2d2d;
  color: #dcdcdc;
  padding: 0.8em 0.6em;
}
```

We also colorise the `footer` component:
`./assets/css/Component/footer.css`

```css
.footer {
  border-top: 1px solid #2d2d2d;
  background-color: #dedede;
  padding: 0.4em 0.6em;
}
```

and the `file-list` component:

`./assets/css/Component/file-list.css`

```
.file-list {
  background-color: #f9f9f9;
  color:  #333341;
}
```

and eventually the `dir-list` component:

`./assets/css/Component/dir-list.css`

```
.dir-list {
  background-color: #dedede;
  color: #ffffff;
  border-right: 1px solid #2d2d2d;
}
```

Now, we only need to include all the modules in the index file:

`./assets/css/app.css:`

```
@import url("./Base/base.css");
@import url("./Component/l-app.css");
@import url("./Component/titlebar.css");
@import url("./Component/footer.css");
@import url("./Component/dir-list.css");
@import url("./Component/file-list.css");
```

As it's done, we launch the application using the following command:

```
npm start
```

It launches the application and shows the layout:

For font sizes and related parameters such as padding, we use relative units (em). It means that we set these values relative to the parent font size:

```
.component { font-size: 10px; } .component__part { font-
size: 1.6em; /* computed font-size is 10*1.6=16px */ }
```

This trick allows us to efficiently scale components. For example, when using the **Responsive Web Design** (**RWD**) approach, we may need to reduce the font sizes and spacing proportionally for a smaller viewport width. When using ems, we just change font size for a target component, and values of subordinated rules will adapt.

Defining CSS variables

NW.js releases quite frequently, basically updating with every new version of Chromium. That means we can safely use the latest CSS features. The one I'm most excited about is called **Custom Properties** (https://www.w3.org/TR/css-variables), which were formerly known as CSS variables.

Actually, variables are one of the main reasons CSS preprocessors exist. With NW.js, we can set variables natively in CSS, as follows:

```
--color-text: #8da3c5;
--color-primary: #189ac4;
```

After that, we can use the variable instead of real values across all the modules in the document scope:

```
.post__title {
  color: var(--color-primary);
}
.post__content {
  color: var(--color-text);
}
```

So if we decide now to change one of defined colors, we need to do it once, and any rules relying on the variable receives the new value. Let's adopt this technology for our application.

First, we need to create definitions for the module:

`./assets/css/Base/defenitions.css`

```
:root {
  --titlebar-bg-color: #2d2d2d;
  --titlebar-fg-color: #dcdcdc;
  --dirlist-bg-color: #dedede;
  --dirlist-fg-color: #636363;
  --filelist-bg-color: #f9f9f9;
  --filelist-fg-color: #333341;
  --dirlist-w: 250px;
  --titlebar-h: 40px;
  --footer-h: 40px;
  --footer-bg-color: #dedede;
  --separator-color: #2d2d2d;
}
```

Here, we define variables representing colors and fixed sizes in the root scope. This new file gets included to the CSS index file:

`./assets/css/app.css:`

```
@import url("./Base/defenitions.css");
...
```

Then, we have to modify our components. First we take care of the top level application layout:

```
./assets/css/Component/l-app.css
```

```css
.l-app {
  display: flex;
  flex-flow: column nowrap;
  align-items: stretch;
}

.l-app__titlebar {
  flex: 0 0 var(--titlebar-h);
}

.l-app__main {
  flex: 1 1 auto;
}

.l-app_footer {
  flex: 0 0 var(--footer-h);
}
```

Then we layout the main section that consists of two columns with dir and file lists:

```
./assets/css/Component/l-main.css
```

```css
.l-main {
  display: flex;
  flex-flow: row nowrap;
  align-items: stretch;
}

.l-main__dir-list {
  flex: 0 0 var(--dirlist-w);
}

.l-main__file-list {
  flex: 1 1 auto;
}
```

We style the header:

`./assets/css/Component/titlebar.css`

```
.titlebar {
  background-color: var(--titlebar-bg-color);
  color: var(--titlebar-fg-color);
  padding: 0.8em 0.6em;
}
```

And the footer:

`./assets/css/Component/footer.css`

```
.footer {
  border-top: 1px solid var(--separator-color);
  background-color: var(--footer-bg-color);
  padding: 0.4em 0.6em;
}
```

We also need to set colors for the child components of the main section. So style the file list component:

`./assets/css/Component/file-list.css`

```
.file-list {
  background-color: var(--filelist-bg-color);
  color: var(--filelist-fg-color);
}
```

and directory list component:

`./assets/css/Component/dir-list.css`

```
.dir-list {
  background-color: var(--dirlist-bg-color);
  color: var(--dirlist-fg-color);
  border-right: 1px solid var(--separator-color);
}
```

We can run the application to observe that it looks the same. All the colors and sizes are successfully extrapolated from the variables.

Sticking the title bar and header

The layout looks fine without any content, but what happens to the layout if it receives content that is too long?

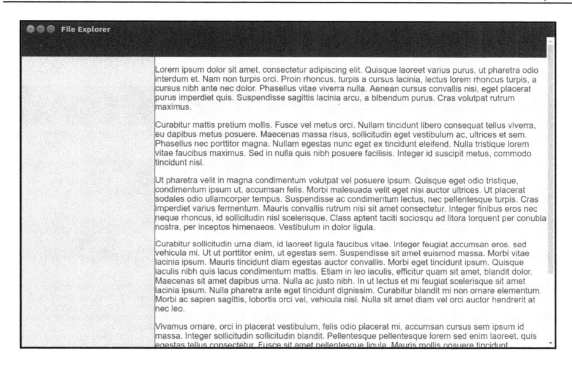

In fact, we will have a header and footer shifting out of the view when scrolling. It doesn't look user-friendly. Fortunately, we can change it easily using another fresh addition to CSS called **Sticky positioning** (https://www.w3.org/TR/css-position-3/#sticky-pos).

All we need to do is to modify slightly the title bar component:

./assets/css/Component/titlebar.css

```
.titlebar {
  ...
  position: sticky;
  top: 0;
}
```

and the footer:

./assets/css/Component/footer.css

```
.footer {
  ...
  position: sticky;
  bottom: 0;
}
```

In the preceding code, we declared that the title bar will stick to the top and footer to the bottom. Run the application now, and you will note that both boxes are always visible, regardless of scrolling:

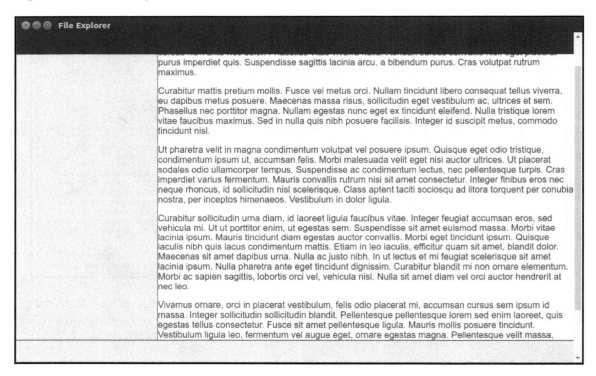

Styling the title bar

Speaking of the view content, we are ready to populate the layout slots. We will start with the title bar:

./index.html

```
<header class="l-app__titlebar titlebar">
  <span class="titlebar__path">/home/sheiko/Sites/file-explorer</span>
  <a class="titlebar__btn" >_</a>
  <a class="titlebar__btn is-hidden" >⊠</a>
  <a class="titlebar__btn" ></a>
  <a class="titlebar__btn" ></a>
</header>
```

Basically, we want the current path to be displayed on the left and window controls on the right. It can be achieved with Flexbox. It's a tiny layout that won't be reused, so it won't hurt if we mix it in the component module:

`./assets/css/Component/titlebar.css`

```
.titlebar {
  ...
  display: flex;
  flex-flow: row nowrap;
  align-items: stretch;
}
.titlebar__path {
  flex: 1 1 auto;
}
.titlebar__btn {
  flex: 0 0 25px;
  cursor: pointer;
}
```

Styling the directory list

The directory list will be used for navigation through the file system, so we will wrap it with the nav > ul structure:

./index.html

```
<aside class="l-main__dir-list dir-list">
  <nav>
    <ul>
      <li class="dir-list__li">..</li>
      <li class="dir-list__li">assets</li>
      <li class="dir-list__li">js</li>
      <li class="dir-list__li">node_modules</li>
      <li class="dir-list__li">tests</li></ul>
  </nav>
</aside>
```

To support it with styles, we go with the following code:

./assets/css/Component/dir-list.css

```
.dir-list__li {
  padding: 0.8em 0.6em;
  cursor: pointer;
  white-space: nowrap;
  overflow: hidden;
  text-overflow: ellipsis;
}

.dir-list__li:hover {
  background-color: var(--dirlist-bg-hover-color);
  color: var(--dirlist-fg-hover-color);
}
```

Note that we've just introduced a couple of variables. Let's add them in the definitions module:

./assets/css/Base/definitions.css

```
--dirlist-bg-hover-color: #d64937;
--dirlist-fg-hover-color: #ffffff;
```

As we ruin the application we can observe the new contents in the directory list:

Styling a file list

The file list will be represented as a table, but we will build it out of an unordered list. The ./index.html file contains the following code:

```
<main class="l-main__file-list file-list">
  <nav>
    <ul>
      <li class="file-list__li file-list__head">
      <span class="file-list__li__name">Name</span>
      <span class="file-list__li__size">Size</span>
      <span class="file-list__li__time">Modified</span>
      </li>
      <li class="file-list__li">
        <span class="file-list__li__name">index.html</span>
        <span class="file-list__li__size">1.71 KB</span>
        <span class="file-list__li__time">3/3/2017, 15:44:19</span>
      </li>
```

```html
      <li class="file-list__li">
        <span class="file-list__li__name">package.json</span>
        <span class="file-list__li__size">539 B</span>
        <span class="file-list__li__time">3/3/2017, 17:53:19</span>
      </li>
    </ul>
  </nav>
</main>
```

In fact, here **Grid Layout** (https://www.w3.org/TR/css3-grid-layout/) would probably suit better; however, at the time of writing, this CSS module was not yet available in NW.js. So, we go on again with Flexbox:

./assets/css/Component/file-list.css

```css
.file-list {
  background-color: var(--filelist-bg-color);
  color: var(--filelist-fg-color);
  cursor: pointer;
}

.file-list__li {
  display: flex;
  flex-flow: row nowrap;
}

.file-list__li:not(.file-list__head){
  cursor: pointer;
}
.file-list__li:not(.file-list__head):hover {
  color: var(--filelist-fg-hover-color);
}
.file-list__li > * {
  flex: 1 1 auto;
  padding: 0.8em 0.8em;
  overflow: hidden;
}

.file-list__li__name {
  white-space: nowrap;
  text-overflow: ellipsis;
  width: 50%;
}
.file-list__li__time {
  width: 35%;
}
.file-list__li__size {
  width: 15%;
```

```
}
```

I believe that everything is clear with the preceding code, except that you might not be familiar with the `pseudo-class :not()`. I want to change the color and mouse cursor on hover for all the file list items, except the table header. So, I achieve it with a selector that can be read like any `.file-list__li` that is not `.file-list__head`.

The following assignment goes to the definitions file:

`./assets/css/Base/definitions.css`

```
--filelist-fg-hover-color: #d64937;
```

As we run the application we can see the table with the file list:

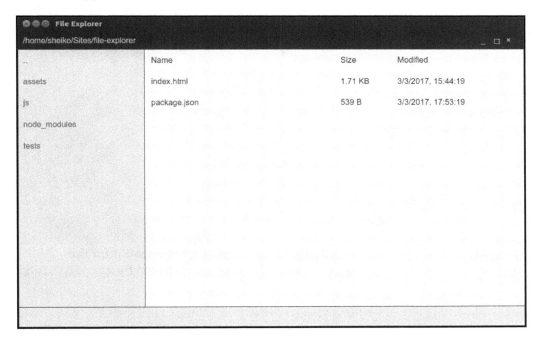

Styling the footer

Eventually, we now reached the footer:

`./index.html`

```
...
<footer class="l-app__footer footer">
  <h2 class="footer__header">File Explorer</h2>
  <select class="footer__select">
    <option value="en-US">English</option>
    <option value="de-DE">Deutsch</option>
  </select>
</footer>
```

We arrange the application title to the left and language selector to the right. What do we use to lay this out? Obviously, Flexbox:

`./assets/css/Component/footer.css`

```
.footer {
  ...
  display: flex;
  flex-flow: row nowrap;
  justify-content: flex-end;
}

.footer__header {
  margin: 0.2em auto 0 0;
  font-size: 1em;
}
```

It's a special case. We set items to align right in general, but have reset it for the `.footer__header` item that snuggles against the left border driven by `margin-right: auto`:

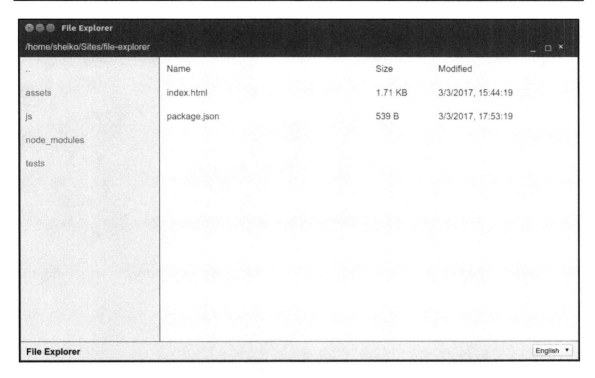

While looking at the result, I think it would be nice to emphasize the functional meaning of some UI elements with icons. I personally prefer the icon font of **Material Design system** (https://material.io/icons/). So, as described in the Developer Guide (http://google.github.io/material-design-icons/), we include the corresponding Google Web Font to index.html:

./index.html

```
<link href="https://fonts.googleapis.com/icon?family=Material+Icons"
      rel="stylesheet">
```

I would suggest that you dedicate a component that will represent an icon and fill it with the rule set suggested by Material Design:

./assets/css/Component/icon.css

```
.icon {
  font-family: 'Material Icons';
  font-weight: normal;
  font-style: normal;
  font-size: 16px;
  display: inline-block;
```

```
    line-height: 1;
    text-transform: none;
    letter-spacing: normal;
    word-wrap: normal;
    white-space: nowrap;
    direction: ltr;
    -webkit-font-smoothing: antialiased;
    text-rendering: optimizeLegibility;
}
```

Now, we can add an icon anywhere in HTML, as simple as that:

```
<i class="material-icons">thumb_up</i>
```

Why not then make a folder icon accompanying items in the directory list?:

```
<li class="dir-list__li"><i class="icon">folder</i>assets</li>
```

I believe that a globe icon will get along nicely with the language selector. So we modify the HTML:

`./index.html`

```
...
<footer class="l-app__footer footer">
    <h2 class="footer__header">File Explorer</h2>
    <label class="icon footer__label">language</label>
        ....
```

and we add a class in the CSS:

`./assets/css/Component/footer.css`

```
...
.footer__label {
  margin-right: 0.2em;
  font-size: 1.4em;
  margin-top: 0.1em;
}
```

As we run the application we can see an icon rendered next to the language selector control:

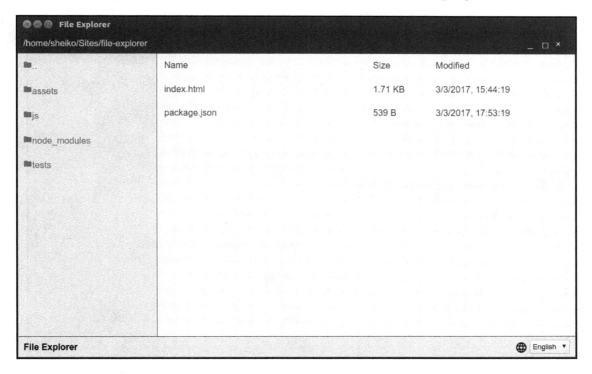

If something went wrong after running the application, you can always call for **Developer Tools**--just press *F12*:

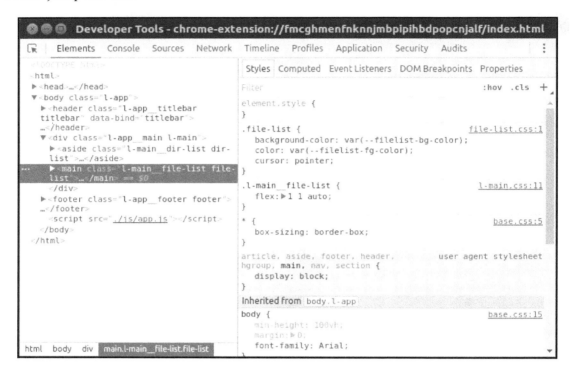

Fulfilling the functional requirements

We've described the semantic structure of our application with HTML. We have defined with CSS how our UI elements shall look. Now, we will teach our application to retrieve and update the content as well as to respond to user events. Actually, we will allocate the following tasks to several modules:

- DirService: This provides control on directory navigation
- FileService: This handles file operations
- FileListView: This updates the file list with the data received from DirService, handles user events (open file, delete file, and so on) using FileService
- DirListView: This updates the directory list with the data received from DirService and handles navigation events using DirService

- `TitleBarPath`: This updates the current location with the path received from DirService
- `TitleBarActions`: This handles user iteration with title bar buttons
- `LangSelector`: This handles user iteration with language selector

However, before we start coding, let's see what we have in our arsenal.

NW.js gets distributed together with the latest stable version of Node.js, which has a great support for ES2015/ES2016 (`http://node.green`). It means that we can use any of the inherent new JavaScript features, but modules (`http://bit.ly/2moblwB`). Node.js has its own CommonJS-compliant module loading system. When we request a module by path, for example, `require( "./foo" )`, the runtime searches for a corresponding file (`foo.js`, `foo.json`, or `foo.node`) or a directory (`./foo/index.js`). Then, Node.js evaluates the module code and returns the exported type.

For example, we can create a module that exports a string:

`./foo.js`

```
console.log( "foo runs" );
exports.message = "foo's export";
```

and another one, which imports from the first module:

`./bar.js`

```
const foo = require( "./foo" );
console.log( foo.message );
```

If we run it, we get the following:

```
$node bar.js
foo runs
foo's export
```

One should note here that regardless of how many times we require a module, it gets executed just once, and every time, its exports are taken from the cache.

Starting with ES2015

As I have already mentioned, NW.js provides a complete support of JavaScript of ES2015 and ES2016 editions. To understand what it really means, we need a brief excursion into the history of the language. The standardized specification for JavaScript was first released in 1997 (ECMA-262 1st Edition).

Since then, the language has not really changed for 10 years. The 4th edition proposed in 2007 called for drastic changes. However, the working group (TC39) failed to agree on the feature set. Some proposals have been deemed unsound for the Web, but some were adopted in a new project code named Harmony. The project turned into the 6th edition of the language specification and was released in 2015 under the official name ES2015. Now, the committee is releasing a new specification every year.

New JavaScript is backward compatible with an earlier version. So, you can still write code with the syntax of the ECMAScript 5th edition or even 3rd one, but why should we lose the opportunity to work with the new advanced syntax and feature set? I think it would be helpful if we now go through some new language aspects that will be used in the application.

Scoping

In the old days, we used to always go with the var statement for variable declarations. ES2015 introduces two new declaration variables--let and const. The var statement declares a variable in a function scope:

```
(function(){
    var foo = 1;
    if ( true ) {
            var foo = 2;
            console.log( foo );
    }
    console.log( foo );
}());

$ node es6.js
2
2
```

A variable declared with var (foo) spans the entire function scope, meaning that every time we reference it by name, we target the same variable. Both let and const operate on block scopes (if statement, for/while loops, and so on) as shown:

```
(function(){
    let foo = 1;
    if ( true ) {
            let foo = 2;
            console.log( foo );
    }
    console.log( foo );
}());
```

```
$ node es6.js
2
1
```

As you can see from the preceding example, we can declare a new variable in a block and it will exist only within that block. The statement `const` works the same, except it defines a constant that cannot be reassigned after it was declared.

Classes

JavaScript implies a prototype-based, object-oriented programming style. It differs from class-based OOP that is used in other popular programming languages, such as C++, C#, Objective-C, Java, and PHP. This used to confuse newcomer developers. ES2015 offers a syntactic sugar over the prototype, which looks pretty much like canonical classes:

```
class Machine {
    constructor( name ){
    this.name = name;
  }
}
class Robot extends Machine {
  constructor( name ){
    super( name );
  }
  move( direction = "left" ){
    console.log( this.name + " moving ", Robot.normalizeDirection( direction
) );
  }
  static normalizeDirection( direction ) {
        return direction.toLowerCase();
  }
}

const robot = new Robot( "R2D2" );
robot.move();
robot.move( "RIGHT" );

$ node es6.js
R2D2 moving  left
R2D2 moving  right
```

Here, we declare a `Machine` class that during instantiation assigns a value to a prototype property, `name`. A `Robot` class extends `Machine` and, therefore, inherits the prototype. In subtype, we can invoke the parent constructor with the `super` keyword.

We also define a prototype method--`move`--and a static method--`normalizeDirection`. The `move` method has a so-called **default function parameter**. So, if we omit the direction argument while calling move method, the parameter automatically sets to `"left"`.

In ES2015, we can use a short syntax for the methods and do not need to repeat function keywords with every declaration. It's also available for object literals:

```
const R2D2 = {
    name: "R2D2",
    move(){
            console.log( "moving" );
    },
    fly(){
            console.log( "flying" );
    }
};
```

The template literal

Another great addition to JavaScript is **template literals**. These are string literals that can be multiline and can include interpolated expressions (`` `${expression}` ``). For example, we can refactor our move method body, as follows:

```
console.log( `
    ${this.name} moving  ${Robot.normalizeDirection( direction )}
` );
```

Getters and setters

Getters and setters were added back in ES5.1. In ES2015, it was extended for computed property names and goes hand in hand with a short method notation:

```
class Robot {
  get nickname(){
    return "But you have to prove first that you belong to the Rebel
        Alliance!";
  }
  set nickname( nickname ){
    throw new Error( "Seriously?!" );
  }
};
```

```
const robot = new Robot();
console.log( robot.nickname );
robot.nickname = "trashcan";

$ node es6.js
But you have to prove first that you belong to the Rebel Alliance!
Error: Seriously?!
```

Arrow functions

A function declaration also obtained syntactic sugar. We write it now with a shorter syntax. It's remarkable that a function defined this way (fat arrow function) automatically picks up the surrounding context:

```
class Robot extends Machine {
   //...
   isRebel(){
          const ALLOWED_NAMES = [ "R2D2", "C3PO" ];
          return ALLOWED_NAMES.find(( name ) => {
                 return name === this.name;
          });
   }
}
```

When using old function syntax, the callback function passed to an array's method, find, would lose the context of the Robot instance. Arrow functions, though, do not create their own context and, therefore, outer context (this) gets in the closure.

In this particular example, as it often goes with array extras, the callback body is extremely short. So, we can use an even shorter syntax:

```
return ALLOWED_NAMES.find( name => name === this.name );
```

Destructuring

In new JavaScript, we can extract specific data from arrays and objects. Let's say, we have an array that could be built by an external function, and we want its first and second elements. We can extract them as simple as this:

```
const robots =  [ "R2D2", "C3PO", "BB8" ];
const [ r2d2, c3po ] = robots;
console.log( r2d2, c3po );
```

So here, we declare two new constants--r2d2 and c3po--and assign the first and the second array elements to them, respectively.

We can do the same with objects:

```
const meta = {
    occupation: "Astromech droid",
    homeworld: "Naboo"
};

const { occupation, homeworld } = meta;
console.log( occupation, homeworld );
```

What did we do? We declared two constants--occupation and homeworld--that receive values from correspondingly named object members.

What is more, we can even alias an object member while extracting:

```
const { occupation: affair, homeworld: home } = meta;
console.log( affair, home );
```

In the last example, we delegated the values of object members--occupation and homeworld--to newly created constants--affair and home.

Handling windowing actions

Coming back to the file-explorer, we can start with the TitleBarActions module that listens to user click events on title bar buttons and performs the corresponding windowing action. First, we need to mark the action nodes in HTML. The ./index.html file contains the following code:

```
<header class="l-app__titlebar titlebar" data-bind="titlebar">
   ...
   <a class="titlebar__btn" data-bind="close" >×</a>
</header>
```

Here, we specify our bounding box (data-bind="titlebar") and the close window button (data-bind="close"). Let's begin with the only button. The ./js/View/TitleBarActions.js file contains the following code:

```
class TitleBarActionsView {

  constructor( boundingEl ){
    this.closeEl = boundingEl.querySelector( "[data-bind=close]" );
        this.bindUi();
```

```
    }

    bindUi(){
          this.closeEl.addEventListener( "click", this.onClose.bind( this
), false );
      }
    onClose( e ) {
     e.preventDefault();
     nw.Window.get().close();
    }
}
```

```
    exports.TitleBarActionsView = TitleBarActionsView;
```

Here, we define a `TitleBarActionView` class that accepts an HTML element as a parameter. This element represents the view bounding box, meaning that the instance of this class will take care only of the passed in element and its descendants. During construction, the class will search for the first element in the scope of the bounding box that matches `selector [data-bind=close]`--the close window button of the title bar. In the `bindUI` method, we subscribe for clicks events on the Close button. When the button is clicked, the `onClose` method is called in the context of a `TitleBarActionView` instance, as we bound it in `bindUi (this.onClose.bind( this ))`. The `onClose` method closes the window using the NW.js Window API (`http://docs.nwjs.io/en/latest/References/Window/`), namely it requests a current window object `nw.Window.get()` and calls its close method.

NW.js doesn't provide a module for the API, but exposes the `nw` variable in the global scope.

So, we have the first view module and can use it the main script:

`./js/app.js`

```
    const { TitleBarActionsView } = require( "./js/View/TitleBarActions" );

    new TitleBarActionsView( document.querySelector( "[data-bind=titlebar]" )
    );
```

Here, we import the `TileBarActionView` class from the `./js/View/TitleBarActions` module and make an instance of it. We pass the first document element matching selector `[data-bind=titlebar]` to the class constructor.

Have you noticed that we used destructuring while importing from the module? Particularly, we extracted the `TitleBarActionsView` class into a respectively called constant.

Now, we can launch the application and observe, as clicking on the close button really closes the window.

Going further, we take care of other title bar buttons. So, we adapt our `index.html` file to identify the buttons, nodes with `unmaximize`, `maximize`, and `minimize` values for the `data-bind` attribute. Then, we collect in the `TileBarActionView` constructor references to the corresponding HTML elements:

```
this.unmaximizeEl = boundingEl.querySelector( "[data-bind=unmaximize]" );
this.maximizeEl = boundingEl.querySelector( "[data-bind=maximize]" );
this.minimizeEl = boundingEl.querySelector( "[data-bind=minimize]" );
```

Of course, we have to add new listeners in the `bindUi` module, respectively:

```
this.minimizeEl.addEventListener( "click", this.onMinimize.bind( this ),
false );
this.maximizeEl.addEventListener( "click", this.onMaximize.bind( this ),
false );
this.unmaximizeEl.addEventListener( "click", this.onUnmaximize.bind( this
), false );
```

The handler for minimizing the window button looks pretty much the same as the one we have already examined previously. It just uses the corresponding method of the NW.js Window API:

```
onMinimize( e ) {
    e.preventDefault();
    nw.Window.get().minimize();
}
```

With maximize and minimize (restore) window buttons, we need to take the fact that while one button is visible the second one shall be hidden into account. This we achieve with the `toggleMaximize` method:

```
toggleMaximize(){
    this.maximizeEl.classList.toggle( "is-hidden" );
    this.unmaximizeEl.classList.toggle( "is-hidden" );
}
```

Event handler for these buttons calls this method to the toggle buttons view:

```
onUnmaximize( e ) {
    e.preventDefault();
    nw.Window.get().unmaximize();
    this.toggleMaximize();
}
onMaximize( e ) {
```

```
    e.preventDefault();
    nw.Window.get().maximize();
    this.toggleMaximize();
}
```

Writing a service to navigate through directories

Other modules, such as `FileListView`, `DirListView`, and `TitleBarPath`, consume the data from the filesystem, such as directory list, file list, and the current path. So we need to create a service that will provide this data:

`./js/Service/Dir.js`

```
const fs = require( "fs" ),
      { join, parse } = require( "path" );

class DirService  {

  constructor( dir = null ){
    this.dir = dir || process.cwd();
  }

  static readDir( dir ) {
    const fInfoArr = fs.readdirSync( dir, "utf-8" ).map(( fileName ) => {
      const filePath = join( dir, fileName ),
            stats = DirService.getStats( filePath );
      if ( stats === false ) {
        return false;
      }
      return {
        fileName,
        stats
      };
    });
    return fInfoArr.filter( item => item !== false );
  }

  getDirList() {
    const collection = DirService.readDir( this.dir ).filter(( fInfo )
        => fInfo.stats.isDirectory() );
    if ( !this.isRoot() ) {
      collection.unshift({ fileName: ".." });
    }
    return collection;
```

```
    }

    getFileList() {
      return DirService.readDir( this.dir ).filter(( fInfo ) =>
        fInfo.stats.isFile() );
    }

    isRoot(){
      const { root } = parse( this.dir );
      return ( root === this.dir );
    }

    static getStats( filePath ) {
      try {
        return fs.statSync( filePath );
      } catch( e ) {
        return false;
      }
    }

};

exports.DirService = DirService;
```

First of all, we import Node.js core module `fs` that provides us access to the filesystem. We also extract functions--`join` and `parse`--from the `path` module. We will need them for manipulations in the file/directory path.

Then, we declare the `DirService` class. On construction, it creates a `dir` property, which takes either a passed-in value or the current working directory (`process.cwd()`). We add a static method--`readDir`--to the class that reads the directory content on a given location. The `fs.readdirSync` method retrieves the content of a directory, but we extend the payload with file/directory stats (`https://nodejs.org/api/fs.html#fs_class_fs_stats`). In case the stats cannot be obtained, we replace its array element with `false`. To avoid such gaps in the output array, we will run the array `filter` method. Thus, on the exit point, we have a clean array of filenames and file stats.

The `getFileList` method requests `readDir` for the current directory content and filters the list to leave only files in there.

The `getDirList` method filters, evidently, the list for directories only. Besides, it prepends the list with a `..` directory for upward navigation, but only if we are not in the system root.

So, we can get both lists from the modules consuming them. When the location changes and new directory and file lists get available, each of these modules have to update. To implement it, we will use the observe pattern:

`./js/Service/Dir.js`

```
//....
const EventEmitter = require( "events" );

class DirService extends EventEmitter {

  constructor( dir = null ){
   super();
   this.dir = dir || process.cwd();
  }
  setDir( dir = "" ){
   let newDir = path.join( this.dir, dir );
   // Early exit
   if ( DirService.getStats( newDir ) === false ) {
   return;
   }
   this.dir = newDir;
   this.notify();
  }

  notify(){
   this.emit( "update" );
  }
  //...
}
```

We export from events, core module the `EventEmitter` class (`https://nodejs.org/api/events.html`). By extending it with `DirService`, we make the service an event emitter. It gives us the possibility to fire service events and to subscribe on them:

```
dirService.on( "customEvent", () => console.log( "fired customEvent" ));
dirService.emit( "customEvent" );
```

So whenever the `setDir` method is called to change the current location, it fires an event of type `"update"`. Given the consuming modules are subscribed, they respond to the event by updating their views.

Unit-testing a service

We've written a service and assume that it fulfills the functional requirements, but we do not know it for sure, yet. To check it, we will create a unit-test.

We do not have any test environment so far. I would suggest going with the **Jasmine** test framework (`https://jasmine.github.io/`). We will create in our `tests/unit-tests` subfolder a dedicated NW.js project, which will be used for the testing. This way, we get the runtime environment for tests, identical to what we have in the application.

So we create the test project manifest:

`./tests/unit-tests/package.json`

```
{
  "name": "file-explorer",
  "main": "specs.html",
  "chromium-args": "--mixed-context"
}
```

It points at the Jasmine test runner page, the one we placed next to `package.json`:

`./tests/unit-tests/specs.html`

```
<!doctype html>
<html>
<head>
    <meta charset="utf-8">
    <title>Jasmine Spec Runner</title>
    <link rel="stylesheet" type="text/css"
href="https://cdnjs.cloudflare.com/ajax/libs/jasmine/2.5.2/jasmine.css">
    <script
src="https://cdnjs.cloudflare.com/ajax/libs/jasmine/2.5.2/jasmine.js"></scr
ipt>
    <script
src="https://cdnjs.cloudflare.com/ajax/libs/jasmine/2.5.2/jasmine-
    html.js"></script>
    <script
src="https://cdnjs.cloudflare.com/ajax/libs/jasmine/2.5.2/boot.js"></script
>
</head>
<body>
  <div id="sandbox" style="display: none"></div>
    <script>
      // Catch exception and report them to the console.
      process.on( "uncaughtException", ( err ) => console.error( err ) );
      const path = require( "path" ),
```

```
                    jetpack = require( "fs-jetpack" ),
                    matchingSpecs = jetpack.find( "../../js", {
                        matching: [
                          "*.spec.js",
                          "!node_modules/**"
                        ]
                    }, "relativePath" );

             matchingSpecs.forEach(( file ) => {
                require( path.join( __dirname, file ) );
             });
        </script>
  </body>
</html>
```

What does this runner do? It loads Jasmine, and with help of the `fs-jetpack` npm module (`https://www.npmjs.com/package/fs-jetpack`), it traverses the source directory recursively for all the files matching `"*.spec.js"` pattern. All these files get added to the test suite. Thus, it assumes that we keep our test specifications next to the target source modules.

`fs-jetpack` is an external module, and we need to install the package and add it to the development dependencies list:

npm i -D fs-jetpack

Jasmine implements a wide-spread, frontend development testing paradigm **Behavior-driven Development (BDD)** that can be described with the following pattern:

```
describe( "a context e.g. class or module", () => {
  describe( "a context e.g. method or function", () => {
    it( "does what expected", () => {
       expect( returnValue ).toBe( expectedValue );
    });
  });
});
```

As it is generally accepted in unit testing, a suite may have setup and teardown:

```
beforeEach(() => {
  // something to run before to every test
});
afterEach(() => {
  // something to run after to every test
});
```

When testing a service that touches the filesystem or communicates across the network or talks to databases, we have to be careful. A good unit test is independent from the environment. So, to test our `DirService`, we have to mock the filesystem. Let's test the `getFileList` method of the service class to see it in action:

`./js/Service/Dir.spec.js`

```
const { DirService } = require( "./Dir" ),
      CWD = process.cwd(),
      mock = require( "mock-fs" ),
      { join } = require( "path" );

describe( "Service/Dir", () => {

  beforeEach(() => {
    mock({
      foo: {
        bar: {
          baz: "baz", // file contains text baz
          qux: "qux"
        }
      }
    });
  });
  afterEach( mock.restore );

  describe( "#getFileList", () => {
    it( "receives intended file list", () => {
      const service = new DirService( join( "foo", "bar" ) );
      service.setDir( "bar" );
      let files = service.getFileList();
      expect( files.length ).toBe( 2 );
    });
    it( "every file has expected properties", () => {
      const service = new DirService( join( "foo", "bar" ) );
      const files = service.getFileList();
      console.log( files );
      const [ file ] = files;
      expect( file.fileName ).toBe( "baz" );
      expect( file.stats.size ).toBe( 3 );
      expect( file.stats.isFile() ).toBe( true );
      expect( file.stats.isDirectory() ).toBe( false );
      expect( file.stats.mtime ).toBeTruthy();
    });
  });
});
```

Before running a test, we point the `fs` method to a virtual filesystem with the folder `/foo/bar/` that contains the `baz` and `qux` files. After every test, we restore access to the original filesystem. In the first test, we instantiate the service on the `foo/bar` location and read the content with the `getFileList()` method. We assert the number of found files as 2 (as we defined in `beforeEach`). In the second test, we take the first element of the list and assert that it contains the intended filename and stats.

As we use an external npm package (`https://www.npmjs.com/package/mock-fs`) for mocking, we need to install it:

```
npm i -D mock-fs
```

As we came up with the first test suite, we can modify our project manifest file for a proper test runner script. The `./package.json` file contains the following code:

```
{
  ...
  "scripts": {
    ...
    "test": "nw tests/unit-tests"
  },
  ...
}
```

Now, we can run the tests:

```
npm test
```

NW.js will load and render the following screen:

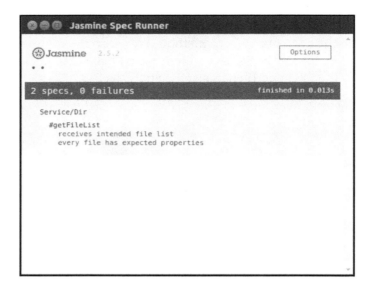

Ideally, unit tests cover all the available functions/methods in the context. I believe that from the preceding code you will get an idea of how to write the tests. However, you may stumble over testing the `EventEmitter` interface; consider this example:

```
describe( "#setDir", () => {
  it( "fires update event", ( done ) => {
    const service = new DirService( "foo" );
    service.on( "update", () => {
      expect( true ).toBe( true );
      done();
    });
    service.notify();
  });
});
```

`EventEmitter` works asynchronously. When we have asynchronous calls in the test body, we shall explicitly inform Jasmin when the test is ready so that the framework could proceed to the next one. That happens when we invoke the callback passed to its function. In the preceding sample, we subscribe the `"update"` event on the service and call `notify` to make it fire the event. As soon as the event is captured, we invoke the `done` callback.

Writing view modules

Well, we have the service, so we can implement the view modules consuming it. However, first we have to mark the bounding boxes for the view in the HTML:

`./index.html`

```html
<span class="titlebar__path" data-bind="path"></span>
..
<aside class="l-main__dir-list dir-list">
  <nav>
    <ul data-bind="dirList"></ul>
  </nav>
</aside>
<main class="l-main__file-list file-list">
  <nav>
    <ul data-bind="fileList"></ul>
  </nav>
</main>
```

The DirList module

What are our requirements for the `DirList` view? It renders the list of directories in the current path. When a user selects a directory from the list, it changes the current path. Subsequently, it updates the list to match the content of the new location:

`./js/View/DirList.js`

```javascript
class DirListView {

  constructor( boundingEl, dirService ){
    this.el = boundingEl;
    this.dir = dirService;
    // Subscribe on DirService updates
    dirService.on( "update", () => this.update( dirService.getDirList() )
);
  }
  onOpenDir( e ){
    e.preventDefault();
    this.dir.setDir( e.target.dataset.file );
  }
  update( collection ) {
    this.el.innerHTML = "";
    collection.forEach(( fInfo ) => {
      this.el.insertAdjacentHTML( "beforeend",
        `<li class="dir-list__li" data-file="${fInfo.fileName}">
```

```
                <i class="icon">folder</i> ${fInfo.fileName}</li>` );
      });
      this.bindUi();
    }
    bindUi(){
      const liArr = Array.from( this.el.querySelectorAll( "li[data-file]" )
);
      liArr.forEach(( el ) => {
        el.addEventListener( "click", e => this.onOpenDir( e ), false );
      });
    }
  }

  exports.DirListView = DirListView;
```

In the class constructor, we subscribe for the DirService "update" event. So, the view gets updated every time the event fired. Method update performs view update. It populates the bounding box with list items built of data received from DirService . As it is done, it calls the bindUi method to subscribe the openDir handler for click events on newly created items. As you may know, Element.querySelectorAll returns not an array, but a non-live NodeList collection. It can be iterated in a for..of loop, but I prefer the forEach array method. That is why I convert the NodeList collection into an array.

The onOpenDir handler method extracts target directory name from the data-file attribute and passes it to DirList in order to change the current path.

Now, we have new modules, so we need to initialize them in app.js:

./js/app.js

```
    const { DirService } = require( "./js/Service/Dir" ),
          { DirListView } = require( "./js/View/DirList" ),
          dirService = new DirService();

    new DirListView( document.querySelector( "[data-bind=dirList]" ),
    dirService );

    dirService.notify();
```

Here, we require new acting classes, create an instance of service, and pass it to the DirListView constructor together with a view bounding box element. At the end of the script, we call dirService.notify() to make all available views update for the current path.

Now, we can run the application and observe as the directory list updates as we navigate through the filesystem:

```
npm start
```

Unit-testing a view module

Seemingly, we are expected to write unit test, not just for services, but for other modules as well. When testing a view we have to check whether it renders correctly in response to specified events:

./js/View/DirList.spec.js

```
const { DirListView } = require( "./DirList" ),
      { DirService } = require( "../Service/Dir" );

describe( "View/DirList", function(){

  beforeEach(() => {
    this.sandbox = document.getElementById( "sandbox" );
    this.sandbox.innerHTML = `<ul data-bind="dirList"></ul>`;
  });

  afterEach(() => {
    this.sandbox.innerHTML = ``;
  });

  describe( "#update", function(){
    it( "updates from a given collection", () => {
      const dirService = new DirService(),
            view = new DirListView( this.sandbox.querySelector( "[data-
bind=dirList]" ), dirService );
      view.update([
        { fileName: "foo" }, { fileName: "bar" }
      ]);
      expect( this.sandbox.querySelectorAll( ".dir-list__li" ).length
).toBe( 2 );
    });
  });
});
```

If you might remember in the test runner HTML, we had a hidden div element with sandbox for id. Before every test, we populate that element with the HTML fragment the view expects. So, we can point the view to the bounding box with the sandbox.

After creating a view instance, we can call its methods, supplying them with an arbitrary input data (here, a collection to update from). At the end of a test, we assert whether the method produced the intended elements within the sandbox.

In the preceding test for simplicity's sake, I injected a fixture array straight to the update method of the view. In general, it would be better to stub `getDirList` of `DirService` using the **Sinon** library (`http://sinonjs.org/`). So, we could also test the view behavior by calling the notify method of `DirService`--the same as it happens in the application.

The FileList module

The module handling the file list works pretty similar to the one we have just examined previously:

`./js/View/FileList.js`

```
const filesize = require( "filesize" );

class FileListView {
  constructor( boundingEl, dirService ){
    this.dir = dirService;
    this.el = boundingEl;
    // Subscribe on DirService updates
    dirService.on( "update", () => this.update(
    dirService.getFileList() ) );
  }
  static formatTime( timeString ){
    const date = new Date( Date.parse( timeString ) );
    return date.toDateString();
  }

  update( collection ) {
    this.el.innerHTML = `<li class="file-list__li file-list__head">
       <span class="file-list__li__name">Name</span>
       <span class="file-list__li__size">Size</span>
       <span class="file-list__li__time">Modified</span>
     </li>`;
    collection.forEach(( fInfo ) => {
      this.el.insertAdjacentHTML( "beforeend", `<li class="file-
          list__li" data-file="${fInfo.fileName}">
       <span class="file-list__li__name">${fInfo.fileName}</span>
       <span class="file-
list__li__size">${filesize(fInfo.stats.size)}</span>
       <span class="file-list__li__time">${FileListView.formatTime(
          fInfo.stats.mtime )}</span>
```

```
      </li>` );
    });
    this.bindUi();
  }

  bindUi(){
    Array.from( this.el.querySelectorAll( ".file-list__li" )
    ).forEach(( el ) => {
      el.addEventListener( "click", ( e ) => {
        e.preventDefault();
        nw.Shell.openItem( this.dir.getFile( el.dataset.file ) );
      }, false );
    });
  }

}

exports.FileListView = FileListView;
```

In the preceding code, in the constructor, we again subscribed the "update" event, and when it was captured, we run the update method on a collection received from the getFileList method of DirService. It renders the file table header first and then the rows with file information. The passed-in collection contains raw file sizes and modification times. So, we format these in a human-readable form. File size gets beautified with an external module--filesize (https://www.npmjs.com/package/filesize)--and the timestamp we shape up with the formatTime static method.

Certainly, we shall load and initialize the newly created module in the main script:

./js/app.js

```
  const { FileListView } = require( "./js/View/FileList" );
  new FileListView( document.querySelector( "[data-bind=fileList]" ),
  dirService );
```

The title bar path module

So we have a directory and file lists responding to the navigation event, but the current path in the title bar is still not affected. To fix it, we will make a small view class:

./js/View/TitleBarPathView.js

```
  class TitleBarPathView {
    constructor( boundingEl, dirService ){
      this.el = boundingEl;
```

```
      dirService.on( "update", () => this.render( dirService.getDir() ) );
    }
    render( dir ) {
      this.el.innerHTML = dir;
    }
  }

  exports.TitleBarPathView = TitleBarPathView;
```

You can note that the class simply subscribes for an update event and modifies the current path accordingly to `DirService`.

To get it live, we will add the following lines to the main script:

`./js/app.js`

```
  const { TitleBarPathView } = require( "./js/View/TitleBarPath" );
  new TitleBarPathView( document.querySelector( "[data-bind=path]" ),
  dirService );
```

Summary

So we've made it to the milestone and have now a working version of the File Explorer providing basic functionality. What have we achieved so far?

We went together though the traditional development routine: we planned, sketched, set up, templated, styled, and programmed. On the way, we discussed the best practices of writing maintainable and conflict-free CSS. We have discovered that NW.js enables the features of the latest CSS and JavaScript specifications. So while refactoring our CSS code, we exploited new aspects, such as custom properties and position sticky. We also had a tour of the basics of ES2015, which helped us to build our JavaScript modules in a cleaner syntax using classes, arrow functions, destructuring, and block scope declarations.

What is more, we explored a few of the goodies normally unavailable in the browser, such as Node.js core and external modules, and the desktop environment integration API. Thus, we were able to access the filesystem and implement windowing actions (close, minimize, maximize, and restore). We made a service extending Node.js EventEmitter and incorporated the event-based architecture to serve our needs.

We didn't forget about unit-testing. We set up Jasmine testing runner and discussed the essentials of BDD specifications. While writing the application unit tests, we examined an approach to mock the filesystem and one to test **Document Object Model (DOM)** manipulations.

Evidently, there's still much left for the second chapter, where we will augment the existing functionality, dive deeper into NW.js API, and go through the preproduction steps. Yet, I hope that you have already accrued a grasp on NW.js and HTML5 desktop development basics. See? It doesn't differ much from traditional web development after all, just unlocks new exciting possibilities.

2
Creating a File Explorer with NW.js – Enhancement and Delivery

Well, we have a working version of File Explorer that can be used to navigate the filesystem and open files with the default associated program. Now we will extend it for additional file operations, such as deleting and copy pasting. These options will keep in a dynamically built context menu. We will also consider the capabilities of NW.js to transfer data between diverse applications using the system clipboard. We will make the application respond to command-line options. We will also provide support for multiple languages and locales. We will protect the sources by compiling them into native code. We will consider packaging and distribution. At the end, we will set up a simple release server and make the File Explorer auto-update.

Internationalization and localization

Internationalization, often abbreviated as **i18n**, implies a particular software design capable of adapting to the requirements of target local markets. In other words, if we want to distribute our application to markets other than the USA, we need to take care of translations, formatting of datetime, numbers, addresses, and such.

Date format by country

Internationalization is a cross-cutting concern. When you are changing the locale, it usually affects multiple modules. So, I suggest going with the observer pattern that we already examined while working on `DirService`:

`./js/Service/I18n.js`

```
const EventEmitter = require( "events" );

class I18nService extends EventEmitter {
  constructor(){

    super();
    this.locale = "en-US";
  }
  notify(){
   this.emit( "update" );
  }
}

exports.I18nService = I18nService;
```

As you see, we can change the `locale` property by setting a new value to the `locale` property. As soon as we call the `notify` method, all the subscribed modules immediately respond.

However, `locale` is a public property and therefore we have no control over its access and mutation. We can fix it using overloading:

`./js/Service/I18n.js`

```
//...
  constructor(){
   super();
   this._locale = "en-US";
  }
  get locale(){

  return this._locale;
  }
  set locale( locale ){
  // validate locale...
   this._locale =

locale;
```

```
    }
    //...
```

Now, if we access the `locale` property of the `I18n` instance, it gets delivered by the getter (`get locale`). When setting it a value, it goes through the setter (`set locale`). Thus, we can add extra functionalities, such as validation and logging on property access and mutation.

Remember that we have a combo box for selecting the language in the HTML. Why not give it a view?

`./js/View/LangSelector.js`:

```js
    class LangSelectorView {
      constructor( boundingEl, i18n ){
       boundingEl.addEventListener( "change",

    this.onChanged.bind( this ), false );
      this.i18n = i18n;
      }
      onChanged( e ){
      const selectEl

    = e.target;
      this.i18n.locale = selectEl.value;
      this.i18n.notify();
      }
    }

    exports.LangSelectorView = LangSelectorView;
```

In the preceding code, we listen for change events on the combo box.

When the event occurs, we change the `locale` property with the passed-in `I18n` instance and call `notify` to inform the subscribers:

`./js/app.js`

```js
    const i18nService = new I18nService(),
        { LangSelectorView } = require( "./js/View/LangSelector" );

    new LangSelectorView( document.querySelector( "[data-bind=langSelector]" ),
    i18nService );
```

Well, we can change the locale and trigger the event. What about consuming modules? In the `FileList` view, we have the `formatTime` static method that formats the passed in `timeString` for printing. We can make it formatted in accordance with the currently chosen `locale`:

`./js/View/FileList.js`:

```
constructor( boundingEl, dirService, i18nService ){
    //...
    this.i18n = i18nService;
    //

Subscribe on i18nService updates
        i18nService.on( "update", () => this.update(
dirService.getFileList() )

);
  }
  static formatTime( timeString, locale ){
    const date = new Date( Date.parse( timeString ) ),

        options = {
        year: "numeric", month: "numeric", day: "numeric",
        hour:

"numeric", minute: "numeric", second: "numeric",
        hour12: false
        };
    return

date.toLocaleString( locale, options );
  }
 update( collection ) {
        //...

this.el.insertAdjacentHTML( "beforeend", `<li class="file-list__li" data-
file="${fInfo.fileName}">

<span class="file-list__li__name">${fInfo.fileName}</span>
        <span class="file-

list__li__size">${filesize(fInfo.stats.size)}</span>
        <span class="file-list__li__time">

${FileListView.formatTime( fInfo.stats.mtime, this.i18n.locale )}</span>
    </li>` );
```

```
//...


  }
//...
```

In the constructor, we subscribe to the `I18n` update event and update the file list every time the locale changes. The `formatTime` static method converts passed the string into a `Date` object and uses the `Date.prototype.toLocaleString()` method to format the datetime according to a given locale. This method belongs to the so called **ECMAScript Internationalization API** (`http://norbertlindenberg.com/2012/12/ecmascript-internalization-api/index.html`). This API describes methods of built-in objects--`String`, `Date`, and `Number`--designed to format and compare localized data. However, what it really does is to format a `Date` instance with `toLocaleString` for the English (United States) locale (`en-US`), and it returns the date, as follows:

```
3/17/2017, 13:42:23
```

However, if we feed German locale (`de-DE`) to the method, we get quite a different result:

```
17.3.2017, 13:42:23
```

To put it into action, we set an identifier to the combo box. The `./index.html` file contains the following code:

```
..
<select class="footer__select" data-bind="langSelector">
..
```

Of course, we have to create an instance of the `I18n` service and pass it in `LangSelectorView` and `FileListView`:

```
./js/app.js
    // ...
    const { I18nService } = require( "./js/Service/I18n" ),
        { LangSelectorView } = require(

    "./js/View/LangSelector" ),
        i18nService = new I18nService();

    new LangSelectorView(

    document.querySelector( "[data-bind=langSelector]" ), i18nService );
    // ...
```

```
new FileListView(

document.querySelector( "[data-bind=fileList]" ), dirService, i18nService
);
```

Now we shall start the application. Yeah! As we change the language in the combo box, the file modification dates are adjusted accordingly:

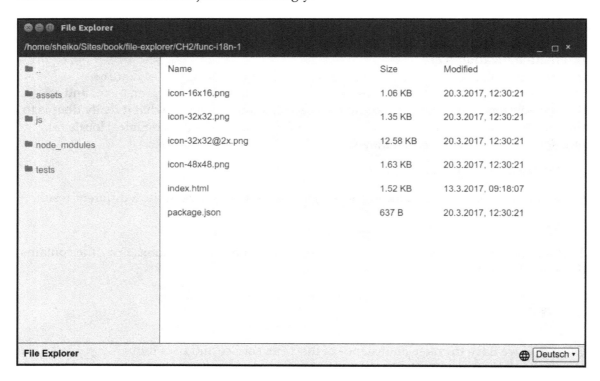

Multilingual support

Localization dates and numbers is a good thing, but it will be more exciting to provide translation to multiple languages. We have a number of terms across the application, namely, the column titles of the file list and tooltips (via the `title` attribute) on windowing action buttons. What we need is a dictionary. Normally, it implies sets of token translation pairs mapped to language codes or locales. Thus, when you request from the translation service a term, it can correlate to a matching translation according to the currently used language/locale.

Here, I have suggested making the dictionary a static module that can be loaded with the required function:

`./js/Data/dictionary.js`

```
exports.dictionary = {
  "en-US": {
    NAME: "Name",
    SIZE: "Size",
    MODIFIED:

"Modified",
    MINIMIZE_WIN: "Minimize window",
    RESTORE_WIN: "Restore window",
    MAXIMIZE_WIN:

"Maximize window",
    CLOSE_WIN: "Close window"
  },
  "de-DE": {
    NAME: "Dateiname",

SIZE: "Grösse",
    MODIFIED: "Geändert am",
    MINIMIZE_WIN: "Fenster minimieren",

RESTORE_WIN: "Fenster wiederherstellen",
    MAXIMIZE_WIN: "Fenster maximieren",
    CLOSE_WIN: "Fenster

schliessen"
  }
};
```

So, we have two locales with translations per term. We will inject the dictionary as a dependency into our I18n service:

`./js/Service/I18n.js`

```
//...
constructor( dictionary ){
    super();
    this.dictionary = dictionary;

this._locale = "en-US";
  }

translate( token, defaultValue ) {
```

```
    const dictionary =
this.dictionary[ this._locale ];
    return dictionary[ token ] || defaultValue;
}
//...
```

We also added a new method, translate, that accepts two parameters: `token` and `default` translation. The first parameter can be one of the keys from the dictionary, such as `NAME`. The second one is guarding value for the case when the requested token does not yet exist in the dictionary. Thus, we still get a meaningful text, at least in English.

Let's look at how we can use this new method:

`./js/View/FileList.js`

```
//...
update( collection ) {
    this.el.innerHTML = `<li class="file-list__li file-list__head">
        <span class="file-list__li__name">${this.i18n.translate( "NAME",
"Name" )}</span>

<span class="file-list__li__size">${this.i18n.translate( "SIZE", "Size"
)}</span>
        <span

class="file-list__li__time">${this.i18n.translate( "MODIFIED", "Modified"
)}</span>
    </li>`;
//...
```

We change the hardcoded column titles in the `FileList` view with calls for the `translate` method of the `I18n` instance, which means that every time the view updates, it receives the actual translations. We shall not forget about the `TitleBarActions` view where we have windowing action buttons:

`./js/View/TitleBarActions.js`

```
constructor( boundingEl, i18nService ){
  this.i18n = i18nService;
  //...
  // Subscribe on

i18nService updates
  i18nService.on( "update", () => this.translate() );
}
```

```
translate(){

  this.unmaximizeEl.title = this.i18n.translate( "RESTORE_WIN", "Restore
window" );
  this.maximizeEl.title =

this.i18n.translate( "MAXIMIZE_WIN", "Maximize window" );
  this.minimizeEl.title = this.i18n.translate(

"MINIMIZE_WIN", "Minimize window" );
  this.closeEl.title = this.i18n.translate( "CLOSE_WIN", "Close window" );
}
```

Here we add the `translate` method, which updates button-title attributes with the actual translations. We subscribe for the `i18n` update event to call the method every time a user changes the `locale`:

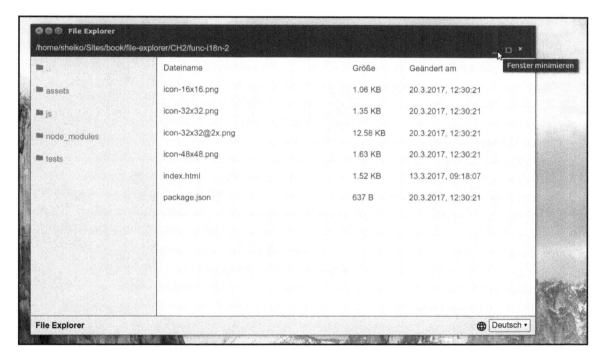

Context menu

Well, with our application, we can already navigate through the filesystem and open files, yet one might expect more of a File Explorer. We can add some file-related actions, such as delete and copy/paste. Usually, these tasks are available via the context menu, which gives us a good opportunity to examine how to make it with NW.js. With the environment integration API, we can create an instance of system menu (http://docs.nwjs.io/en/latest/References/Menu/). Then, we compose objects representing menu items and attach them to the menu instance (http://docs.nwjs.io/en/latest/References/MenuItem/). This menu can be shown in an arbitrary position:

```
const menu = new nw.Menu(),
      menutItem = new nw.MenuItem({
        label: "Say hello",

click: () => console.log( "hello!" )
      });

menu.append( menu );
menu.popup( 10, 10 );
```

Yet, our task is more specific. We have to display the menu on the right-click in the position of the cursor, that is, we achieve it by subscribing a handler to contextmenu DOM event:

```
document.addEventListener( "contextmenu", ( e ) => {
  console.log( `Show menu in position ${e.x}, ${e.y}`
);
});
```

Now, whenever we right-click within the application window, the menu shows up. It's not exactly what we want, is it? We need it only when the cursor resides within a particular region, for instance, when it hovers a file name. This means that we have to test whether the target element matches our conditions:

```
document.addEventListener( "contextmenu", ( e ) => {
  const el = e.target;
  if ( el instanceof

HTMLElement && el.parentNode.dataset.file ) {
    console.log( `Show menu in position ${e.x}, ${e.y}` );


  }
});
```

Here, we ignore the event until the cursor hovers over any cell of the file table row, given that every row is a list item generated by the `FileList` view and therefore provided with a value for a data file attribute.

This passage pretty much explains how to build a system menu and how to attach it to the file list. However, before starting on a module capable of creating a menu, we need a service to handle file operations:

`./js/Service/File.js`

```
const fs = require( "fs" ),
      path = require( "path" ),
      // Copy file helper
      cp = (

from, toDir, done ) => {
        const basename = path.basename( from ),
              to = path.join(

toDir, basename ),
              write = fs.createWriteStream( to ) ;

        fs.createReadStream( from

)
          .pipe( write );

      write
        .on( "finish",  done );
    };



class FileService {

  constructor( dirService ){
    this.dir = dirService;

this.copiedFile = null;
  }
  remove( file ){
    fs.unlinkSync( this.dir.getFile( file ) );
    this.dir.notify();
  }
  paste(){
    const file = this.copiedFile;
    if (
```

```
    fs.lstatSync( file ).isFile() ){
        cp( file, this.dir.getDir(), () => this.dir.notify() );
    }

}

  copy( file ){
    this.copiedFile = this.dir.getFile( file );
  }

  open( file

){
    nw.Shell.openItem( this.dir.getFile( file ) );
  }
  showInFolder( file ){

nw.Shell.showItemInFolder( this.dir.getFile( file ) );
  }
};

exports.FileService =

FileService;
```

What's going on here? `FileService` receives an instance of `DirService` as a constructor argument. It uses the instance to obtain the full path to a file by name (`this.dir.getFile( file )`). It also exploits the `notify` method of the instance to request all the views subscribed to `DirService` to update. The `showInFolder` method calls the corresponding method of `nw.Shell` to show the file in the parent folder with the system file manager. As you can recon, the `remove` method deletes the file. As for copy/paste, we do the following trick. When the user clicks on copy, we store the target file path in the `copiedFile` property. So, when the user clicks on paste the next time, we can use it to copy that file to the supposedly changed current location. The `open` method evidently opens the file with the default associated program. That is what we do in the `FileList` view directly. Actually, this action belongs to `FileService`. So, we adjust the view to use the service:

`./js/View/FileList.js`

```
  constructor( boundingEl, dirService, i18nService, fileService ){
    this.file = fileService;
    //...
  }
  bindUi(){
    //...
```

```
      this.file.open( el.dataset.file );
      //...
   }
```

Now, we have a module to handle the context menu for a selected file. The module will subscribe for the `contextmenu` DOM event and build a menu when the user right-clicks on a file. This menu will contain **Show Item** in the **Folder**, **Copy**, **Paste**, and **Delete**. **Copy** and **Paste** are separated from other items with delimiters, and **Paste** will be disabled until we store a file with **Copy**:

`./js/View/ContextMenu.js`

```
   class ConextMenuView {
      constructor( fileService, i18nService ){
         this.file = fileService;

this.i18n = i18nService;
         this.attach();
      }
      getItems( fileName ){
         const file =

this.file,
             isCopied = Boolean( file.copiedFile );

      return [
         {

label: this.i18n.translate( "SHOW_FILE_IN_FOLDER", "Show Item in the
                                              Folder" ),
            enabled: Boolean( fileName ),


            click: () => file.showInFolder( fileName )
         },
         {
            type: "separator"


         },
         {
            label: this.i18n.translate( "COPY", "Copy" ),
            enabled: Boolean(

                fileName ),
            click: () => file.copy( fileName )
         },
         {
```

```
            label:

this.i18n.translate( "PASTE", "Paste" ),
        enabled: isCopied,
        click: () => file.paste()


    },
    {
      type: "separator"
    },
    {
      label:

this.i18n.translate( "DELETE", "Delete" ),
        enabled: Boolean( fileName ),
        click: () =>

file.remove( fileName )
      }
    ];
  }

  render( fileName ){
    const menu = new

nw.Menu();
    this.getItems( fileName ).forEach(( item ) => menu.append( new
                                        nw.MenuItem( item )));

return menu;
  }

  attach(){
    document.addEventListener( "contextmenu", ( e ) => {

const el = e.target;
      if ( !( el instanceof HTMLElement ) ) {
        return;
      }

      if ( el.classList.contains( "file-list" ) ) {
        e.preventDefault();
        this.render()

        .popup( e.x, e.y );
      }
      // If a child of an element matching [data-file]
```

```
      if (

el.parentNode.dataset.file ) {
        e.preventDefault();
        this.render( el.parentNode.dataset.file )


        .popup( e.x, e.y );
    }

  });
  }
}


    exports.ConextMenuView = ConextMenuView;
```

So, in the `ConextMenuView` constructor, we receive instances of `FileService` and
`I18nService`. During the construction, we also call the `attach` method, which subscribes
for the `contextmenu` DOM event, creates the menu, and shows it in the position of the
mouse cursor. The event gets ignored unless the cursor hovers over a file or resides in the
empty area of the file list component. When the user right-clicks on the file list, the menu
still appears, but with all items disabled except **Paste** (in case a file was copied before).
Method render to create an instance of the menu and populates it with `nw.MenuItems`
created by the `getItems` method. The method creates an array representing menu items.
Elements of the array are object literals. The `label` property accepts translation for item
captions. The `enabled` property defines the state of an item depending on our cases
(whether we hold the copied file or not). Finally, the `click` property expects the handler for
the click event.

Now we need to enable our new components in the main module:

`./js/app.js`

```
  const { FileService } = require( "./js/Service/File" ),
      { ConextMenuView } = require(

  "./js/View/ConextMenu" ),
      fileService = new FileService( dirService );

  new FileListView(

  document.querySelector( "[data-bind=fileList]" ), dirService, i18nService,
  fileService );
  new ConextMenuView(

  fileService, i18nService );
```

Now, let's run the application, right-click on a file, and voila! We have the context menu and new file actions:

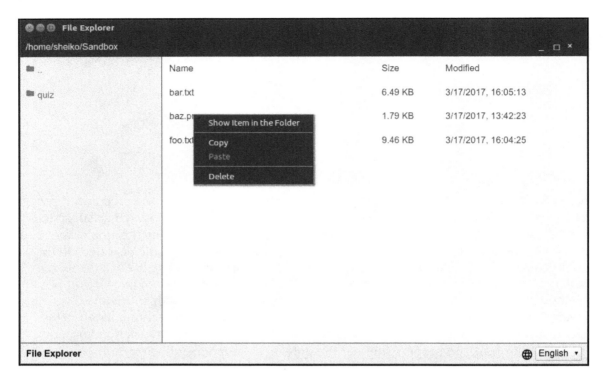

System clipboard

Usually, the copy/paste functionality involves system clipboard. `NW.js` provides an API to control it (`http://docs.nwjs.io/en/latest/References/Clipboard/`). Unfortunately, it's quite limited; we cannot transfer an arbitrary file between applications, which you may expect of a file manager. Yet, some things are still available to us.

Transferring text

In order to examine text transferring with the clipboard, we modify the method copy of `FileService`:

```
copy( file ){
    this.copiedFile = this.dir.getFile( file );
```

```
const clipboard = nw.Clipboard.get();


clipboard.set( this.copiedFile, "text" );
}
```

What does it do? As soon as we obtain the file full path, we create an instance of
`nw.Clipboard` and save the file path there as text. So now, after copying a file within the
File Explorer, we can switch to an external program (for example, a text editor) and paste
the copied path from the clipboard:

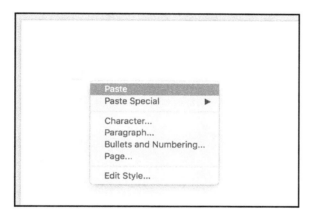

Transferring graphics

It doesn't look very handy, does it? It would be more interesting if we could copy/paste a
file. Unfortunately, `NW.js` doesn't give us many options when it comes to file exchange.
However, we can transfer PNG and JPEG images between the `NW.js` application and
external programs:

`./js/Service/File.js`

```
//...
  copyImage( file, type ){
    const clip = nw.Clipboard.get(),
          // load file content
as Base64
          data = fs.readFileSync( file ).toString( "base64" ),
          // image as HTML
      html = `<img src="file:///${encodeURI( data.replace( /^//, "" ) )}">`;
```

```
    // write both options

(raw image and HTML) to the clipboard
    clip.set([
      { type, data: data, raw: true },
      { type:

"html", data: html }
    ]);
  }
  copy( file ){
    this.copiedFile = this.dir.getFile(

file );
    const ext = path.parse( this.copiedFile ).ext.substr( 1 );
    switch ( ext ){
      case

"jpg":
    case "jpeg":
      return this.copyImage( this.copiedFile, "jpeg" );
    case "png":
      return this.copyImage( this.copiedFile, "png" );
  }
  }
//...
```

We extended our `FileService` with the `copyImage` private method. It reads a given file, converts its contents in Base64 and passes the resulting code in a clipboard instance. In addition, it creates HTML with an image tag with the Base64-encoded image in the data **Uniform Resource Identifier (URI)**. Now, after copying an image (PNG or JPEG) in File Explorer, we can paste it in an external program, such as the graphical editor or text processor.

Receiving text and graphics

We've learned how to pass text and graphics from our `NW.js` application to external programs, but how can we receive data from outside? As you can guess, it is accessible through the `get` method of `nw.Clipboard`. Text can be retrieved as follows:

```
const clip = nw.Clipboard.get();
console.log( clip.get( "text" ) );
```

When the graphic is put on the clipboard, we can get it with NW.js only as Base64-encoded content or as HTML. To see it in practice, we add a few methods to `FileService`:

`./js/Service/File.js`

```
//...
   hasImageInClipboard(){
      const clip = nw.Clipboard.get();
      return

clip.readAvailableTypes().indexOf( "png" ) !== -1;
   }
   pasteFromClipboard(){
      const clip =

nw.Clipboard.get();
      if ( this.hasImageInClipboard() ) {
         const base64 = clip.get( "png", true ),
               binary = Buffer.from( base64, "base64" ),
               filename = Date.now() + "--img.png";

fs.writeFileSync( this.dir.getFile( filename ), binary );
         this.dir.notify();
      }
   }
//...
```

The `hasImageInClipboard` method checks whether the clipboard keeps any graphics. The `pasteFromClipboard` method takes graphical content from the clipboard as a Base64-encoded PNG; it converts the content into binary code, writes it into a file, and requests `DirService` subscribers to update it.

To make use of these methods, we need to edit the `ContextMenu` view:

`./js/View/ContextMenu.js`

```
   getItems( fileName ){
      const file = this.file,
            isCopied = Boolean( file.copiedFile );
         return [
      //...
         {
            label: this.i18n.translate( "PASTE_FROM_CLIPBOARD", "Paste

image from clipboard" ),
            enabled: file.hasImageInClipboard(),
            click: () =>
```

```
file.pasteFromClipboard()
      },
      //...
    ];
  }
```

We add a new item, `Paste image from clipboard`, to the menu, which is enabled only when there are some graphics in the clipboard.

Menu in the system tray

All three platforms available for our application have a so-called system notification area, which is also known as the system tray. That's a part of the user interface (in the bottom-right corner on Windows and top-right corner on other platforms) where you can find the application icon even when it's not present on the desktop. Using the `NW.js` API (`http://docs.nwjs.io/en/latest/References/Tray/`), we can provide our application with an icon and drop-down menu in the tray, but we do not have any icon yet. So, I have created the `icon.png` image with the text `Fe` and saved it in the application root in the size of 32x32px. It is supported on Linux, Windows, and macOS. However, in Linux, we can go with a better resolution, so I have placed the 48x48px version next to it.

Our application in the tray will be represented by `TrayService`:

`./js/View/Tray.js`

```
const appWindow = nw.Window.get();

class TrayView {
  constructor( title ){

this.tray = null;
    this.title = title;
    this.removeOnExit();
    this.render();
  }


  render(){
    const icon = ( process.platform === "linux" ? "icon-48x48.png" :
"icon-32x32.png" );

    this.tray = new nw.Tray({
      title: this.title,
      icon,
```

```
      iconsAreTemplates: false
    });

    const menu = new nw.Menu();
    menu.append( new nw.MenuItem({
      label: "Exit",

      click: () => appWindow.close()
    }));
    this.tray.menu = menu;
  }


removeOnExit(){
    appWindow.on( "close", () => {
      this.tray.remove();
      appWindow.hide();

// Pretend to be closed already
      appWindow.close( true );
    });
    // do not spawn Tray instances

on page reload
    window.addEventListener( "beforeunload", () => this.tray.remove(),
false );
  }

}

exports.TrayView = TrayView;
```

What does it do? The class takes the tray's title as a constructor parameter and calls the
`removeOnExit` and render methods during instantiation. The first one subscribes for the
window's `close` event and ensures that the tray is removed when we close the application.
Method render creates the `nw.Tray` instance. With the constructor argument, we pass the
configuration object with the title, which is a relative path to the icon. We assign it with
`icon- 48x48.png` icon for Linux and `icon-32x32.png` for other platforms. By default,
macOS tries adapting the image to the menu theme, which requires an icon to consist of
clear colors on a transparent background. If your icon doesn't fit these restrictions, you
would rather add it into configuration object property `iconsAreTemplates`, which is set as
`false`.

When launching our File Explorer in Ubuntu 16.x, it doesn't appear in the system tray due to the whitelisting policy. You can fix this by running `sudo apt-get install libappindicator1` in the Terminal.

`nw.Tray` accepts the `nw.Menu` instance. So, we populate the menu the same way as we did for the context menu. Now we just initialize the `Tray` view in the main module and run the application:

`./js/app.js`

```
const { TrayView } = require( "./js/View/Tray" );
new TrayView( "File Explorer" );
```

If we run the application now we can see the app icon and the menu in the system tray:

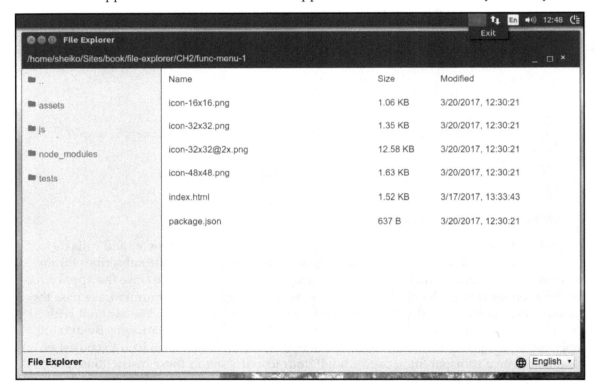

Yes, the only menu item exit looks somehow lonely.

Let's extend the `Tray` view:

`./js/View/Tray.js`

```
class TrayView {
  constructor( title ){
    this.tray = null;
    this.title = title;
    // subscribe to window events
    appWindow.on("maximize", () => this.render( false ));

appWindow.on("minimize", () => this.render( false ));
    appWindow.on("restore", () => this.render( true ));



    this.removeOnExit();
    this.render( true );
  }
  getItems( reset ){

  return [
      {
        label: "Minimize",
        enabled: reset,
        click: () =>

appWindow.minimize()
      },
      {
        label: "Maximize",
        enabled: reset,

    click: () => appWindow.maximize()
      },
      {
        label: "Restore",
        enabled:

!reset,
        click: () => appWindow.restore()
      },
      {
        type: "separator"
      },
      {
        label: "Exit",
        click: () => appWindow.close()
```

```
      }
  ];
  }
  render( reset ){
    if ( this.tray ) {
      this.tray.remove();
    }



    const icon = ( process.platform === "darwin" ? "macicon.png" :
"icon.png" );

    this.tray =

new nw.Tray({
      title: this.title,
      icon,
      iconsAreTemplates: true
    });

    const menu = new nw.Menu();
    this.getItems( reset ).forEach(( item ) => menu.append( new
nw.MenuItem(

item )));

    this.tray.menu = menu;
  }
  removeOnExit(){
    appWindow.on(

"close", () => {
      this.tray.remove();
      appWindow.hide(); // Pretend to be closed already

  appWindow.close( true );
    });
  }

}

exports.TrayView = TrayView;
```

Now, the `render` method receives a Boolean as an argument defining whether the application window is in the initial mode; that flag gets passed to the new `getItems` method that produces an array of menu items meta. If the flag is true, all the menu items are enabled, except restore. What makes sense is to restore the switches window to the initial mode after minimizing or maximizing. Seemingly, when the flag is `false`, the `Minimize` and `Maximize` items are disabled, but how can we know the current mode of the window? While constructing, we subscribe to window events minimize, maximize, and restore. When an event happens, we call `render` with the corresponding flag. Since we can now change window mode from both the `TitleBarActions` and `Tray` views, the `toggle` method of `TitleBarActions` is not a reliable source of window mode anymore. Instead, we rather refactor the module to rely on window events like we did in the `Tray` view:

`./js/View/TitleBarActions.js`

```
const appWindow = nw.Window.get();
class TitleBarActionsView {
  constructor(

boundingEl, i18nService ){
    this.i18n = i18nService;
    this.unmaximizeEl = boundingEl.querySelector(

"[data-bind=unmaximize]" );
    this.maximizeEl = boundingEl.querySelector( "[data-bind=maximize]" );

this.minimizeEl = boundingEl.querySelector( "[data-bind=minimize]" );
    this.closeEl = boundingEl.querySelector(

"[data-bind=close]" );
    this.bindUi();
    // Subscribe on i18nService updates
    i18nService.on(

"update", () => this.translate() );

    // subscribe to window events
    appWindow.on("maximize", ()

=> this.toggleButtons( false ) );
    appWindow.on("minimize", () => this.toggleButtons( false ) );

appWindow.on("restore", () => this.toggleButtons( true ) );
  }
  translate(){

this.unmaximizeEl.title = this.i18n.translate( "RESTORE_WIN", "Restore
window" );
```

```
      this.maximizeEl.title =

this.i18n.translate( "MAXIMIZE_WIN", "Maximize window" );
      this.minimizeEl.title = this.i18n.translate(

"MINIMIZE_WIN", "Minimize window" );
      this.closeEl.title = this.i18n.translate( "CLOSE_WIN", "Close window"
);
    }
   bindUi(){
      this.closeEl.addEventListener( "click", this.onClose.bind( this ),
false );
      this.minimizeEl.addEventListener( "click", this.onMinimize.bind( this
), false );

this.maximizeEl.addEventListener( "click", this.onMaximize.bind( this ),
false );

this.unmaximizeEl.addEventListener( "click", this.onRestore.bind( this ),
false );
    }

toggleButtons( reset ){
      this.maximizeEl.classList.toggle( "is-hidden", !reset );

this.unmaximizeEl.classList.toggle( "is-hidden", reset );
      this.minimizeEl.classList.toggle( "is-hidden", !reset

);
    }
   onRestore( e ) {
     e.preventDefault();
     appWindow.restore();
    }
   onMaximize( e ) {
     e.preventDefault();
     appWindow.maximize();
    }

onMinimize( e ) {
     e.preventDefault();
     appWindow.minimize();
    }
   onClose( e ) {

     e.preventDefault();
     appWindow.close();
```

```
    }
}

exports.TitleBarActionsView =

TitleBarActionsView;
```

This time when we run the application we can find in the system tray application menu with windowing actions:

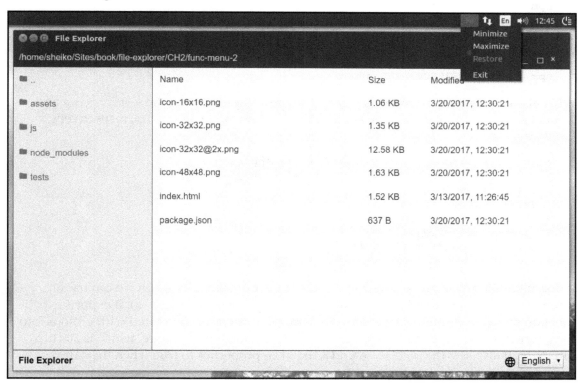

Command-line options

Other file managers usually accept command-line options. For example, you can specify a folder when launching Windows Explorer. It also responds to various switches. Let's say that you can give it switch /e, and Explorer will open the folder in expanded mode.

NW.js reveals command-line options as an array of strings in nw.App.argv. So, we can change the code of the DirService initialization in the main module:

./js/app.js

```
const dirService = new DirService( nw.App.argv[ 0 ] );
```

Now, we can open a specified folder in the File Explorer straight from the command line:

npm start ~/Sandbox

In UNIX-based systems, the tilde means user home directory. The equivalent in Windows will be as follows:

npm start %USERPROFILE%Sandbox

What else can we do? Just for a showcase, I suggest implementing the --minimize and --maximize options that switch the application window mode on startup, respectively:
./js/app.js

```
const argv = require( "minimist" )( nw.App.argv ),
        dirService = new DirService( argv._[ 0 ] );
 if ( argv.maximize ){
  nw.Window.get().maximize();
}
if ( argv.minimize ){
  nw.Window.get().minimize();
}
```

It doesn't make any sense to parse nw.App.argv array manually when we can use an external module minimist (https://www.npmjs.com/package/minimist). It exports a function that collects all the arguments that are not options or associated with options into the _ (underscore) property. We expect the only argument of that type, which is startup directory. It also sets the maximize and minimize properties to true when they are provided on the command line.

One should note that NPM doesn't delegate options to the running script, so we shall call the NW.js executable directly:

nw . ~/Sandbox/ --minimize

or

nw . ~/Sandbox/ --maximize

Native look and feel

Nowadays, one can find plenty of native desktop applications with semi-transparent background or with round corners. Can we achieve such fancy look with NW.js? Sure we can! First, we shall edit our application manifest file:

`./package.json`

```
...
"window": {
    "frame": false,
    "transparent": true,
    ...
},
...
```

By setting the frame field to `false`, we instruct NW.js to not show the window frame, but its contents. Fortunately, we have already implemented custom windowing controls as the default ones will not be available anymore. With a transparent field, we remove the opacity of the application window. To see it in action, we edit the CSS definitions module:

`./assets/css/Base/definitions.css`

```
:root {
  --titlebar-bg-color: rgba(45, 45, 45, 0.7);
  --titlebar-fg-color: #dcdcdc;
  --dirlist-
bg-color: rgba(222, 222, 222, 0.9);
  --dirlist-fg-color: #636363;
  --filelist-bg-color: rgba(249, 249, 249,
0.9);
  --filelist-fg-color: #333341;
  --dirlist-w: 250px;
  --titlebar-h: 40px;
  --footer-h:
40px;
  --footer-bg-color: rgba(222, 222, 222, 0.9);
  --separator-color: #2d2d2d;
  --border-radius:
1em;
}
```

With RGBA color function, we set the opacity of the title bar to 70% and other background colors to 90%. We also introduce a new variable, `--border-radius`, which we will use in the `titlebar` and `footer` components to make round corners on the top and in the bottom:

`./assets/css/Component/titlebar.css`

```
.titlebar {
  border-radius: var(--border-radius) var(--border-radius) 0 0;
}
```

`./assets/css/Component/footer.css`

```
.footer {
  border-radius: 0 0 var(--border-radius) var(--border-radius);
}
```

Now we can launch the application and enjoy our renewed fancy look.

> On Linux, we need to use the `nw . --enable-transparent-visuals --disable-gpu` command-line option to trigger transparency.

Source code protection

Unlike in native applications, our source code isn't compiled and is therefore open to everybody. If you have any commercial use of this fact in mind, it is unlikely to suit you. The least you can do is to obfuscate the source code, for example, using Jscrambler (`https://jscrambler.com/en/`). On the other hand, we can compile our sources into native code and load it with `NW.js` instead of JavaScript. For that, we need to separate JavaScript from the application bundle. Let's create the `app` folder and move everything except `js` there. The `js` folder will be moved into a newly created directory, `src`:

```
.
├── app
│
└── assets
    │       └── css
    │           ├── Base
    │           └──
```

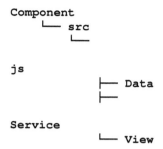

```
Component
    └── src
        └──
```

```
js
            ├── Data
            ├──
```

```
Service
        └── View
```

Our JavaScript modules are now out of the project scope, and we cannot reach them when required. However, these are still Node.js modules (https://nodejs.org/api/modules.html) that confront CommonJS module definition standards. Therefore, we can merge them, with a bundler tool, into a single file that we later compile into native code. I suggest going with Webpack (https://webpack.github.io/), the seemingly most popular bundler nowadays. So, we place it in the root directory webpack configuration file with the following contents:

webpack.config.js

```
const { join } = require( "path" ),
      webpack = require( "webpack" );

module.exports = {

  entry: join( __dirname, "src/js/app.js" ),
    target: "node-webkit",
    output: {
        path: join(

__dirname, "/src/build" ),
        filename:  "bundle.js"
    }
};
```

With this, we instruct Webpack to transpile all the required modules, starting with src/js/app.js, into a single src/build/bundle.js file. However, Webpack, unlike NW.js, expects the required dependencies relative to the hosting file (not project root); so, we have to remove js/ from the file paths in the main module:

./src/js/app.js

```
// require( "./js/View/LangSelector" ) becomes
require( "./View/LangSelector" )
```

For both transpiling CommonJS modules and compiling the derived file in the native code, we need a few tasks in the script field of the manifest:

```
package.json
    //...
    "scripts": {
        "build:js": "webpack",
        "protect:js": "node_modules/nw/nwjs/nwjc

src/build/bundle.js app/app.bin",
        "build": "npm run build:js && npm run protect:js",
        //...
    },
    //...
```

With the first task, we make webpack build our JavaScript sources into a single file. The second one compiles it using the NW.js compiler. The last one does both at once.

In the HTML file, we replace the code calling the main module with the following lines:

```
app/index.html
    <script>
        nw.Window.get().evalNWBin( null, "./app.bin" );
    </script>
```

Now we can run the application and observe that the implemented functionality still confronts our requirements.

Packaging

Well, we have completed our application and that is the time to think about distribution. As you understand, asking our users to install Node.js and type npm start from the command line will not be friendly. Users will expect a package that can be started as simply as any other software. So, we have to bundle our application along with NW.js for every target platform. Here, nwjs-builder comes in handy (https://github.com/evshiron/nwjs-builder).

So, we install the npm i -D nwjs-builder tool and add a task to the manifest:

```
./package.json
    //...
    "scripts": {
```

```
    "package": "nwb nwbuild -v 0.21.3-sdk ./app -o ./dist  -p linux64,
win32,osx64",


    //...
  },
//...
```

Here, we specified three target platforms (-p linux64, win32,osx64) at once and thus, after running this task (npm run package), we get platform-specific subfolders in the dist directory, containing other executable things named after our application:

```
dist
├── file-explorer-linux-x64
│    └── file-explorer


├── file-explorer-osx-x64
│    └── file-explorer.app
└── file-explorer-win-x64
     └── file-explorer.exe
```

Nwjs-builder accepts diverse options. For example, we can request it to output the packages as ZIP archives:

nwb nwbuild -v 0.21.3-sdk ./app -o ./dist --output-format=ZIP

Alternatively, we can make it run the package after the build process with the given options:

nwb nwbuild -v 0.21.3-sdk ./app -o ./dist -r -- --enable-transparent-visuals --disable-gpu

Autoupdate

In the era of continuous deployment, new releases are issued pretty often. As developers, we have to ensure that users receive the updates transparently, without going through the download/install routine. With the traditional web application, it's taken for granted. Users hit the page and the latest version gets loaded. With desktop applications, we need to deliver the update. Unfortunately, NW.js doesn't provide any built-in facilities to handle autoupdates, but we can trick it; let's see how.

First of all, we need a simple release server. Let's give it a folder (for example, `server`) and create the manifest file there:

`./server/package.json`

```json
{
  "name": "release-server",
  "version": "1.0.0",
  "packages": {
    "linux64": {
      "url": "http://localhost:8080/releases/file-explorer-linux-
      x64.zip",
      "size": 98451101
    }
  },
  "scripts": {
    "start": "http-server ."
  }
}
```

This file contains a `packages` custom field, describing the available application releases. This simplified implementation accepts only the latest release per platform. The release version must be set in the manifest version field. Every entry of package objects contains a downloadable URL and the package size in bytes.

To serve HTTP requests for this manifest and packages in the `release` folder, we will use the HTTP server (`https://www.npmjs.com/package/http-server`). So, we install the package and start the HTTP server:

```
npm i -S http-server
npm start
```

Now, we will jump back to our client and modify the application manifest file:

`./client/package.json`

```json
{
  "name": "file-explorer",
  "manifestUrl": "http://127.0.0.1:8080/package.json",
  "scripts": {

    "package": "nwb nwbuild -v 0.21.3-sdk . -o ../server/releases --output-
format=ZIP",
    "postversion": "npm

run package"
```

```
    },
   //...
   }
```

Here, we add a custom field, `manifestUrl`, with a URL to the server manifest. After we start the server, the manifest will be available at
`http://127.0.0.1:8080/package.json`. We instruct `nwjs-builder` to pack application bundles with ZIP and place them in `../server/release`. Eventually, we set the `postversion` hook; so, when bumping the package version (for example, `npm version patch`) NPM will automatically build and send a release package to the server, every time.

From the client, we can read the server manifest and compare it with the application. If the server has a newer version, we download the release package matching our platform and unpack it in a temporary directory. What we need to do now is just replace the running application version with the downloaded one. However, the folder is locked until the app is running, so we close the running application and start the downloaded one (as a detached process). It backs up the old version and copies the downloaded package to the initial location. All that can be easily done using `nw- autoupdater`
(`https://github.com/dsheiko/nw-autoupdater`), so we install the `npm i -D nw-autoupdater` package and create a new service to handle the autoupdate flow:

`./client/js/Service/Autoupdate.js`

```
    const AutoUpdater = require( "nw-autoupdater" ),
        updater = new AutoUpdater( nw.App.manifest );

    async function start( el ){
      try {
        // Update copy is running to replace app with the update
        if

( updater.isSwapRequest() ) {
        el.innerHTML = `Swapping...`;
        await updater.swap();

el.innerHTML = `Restarting...`;
        await updater.restart();
        return;
      }

      //

Download/unpack update if any available
        const rManifest = await updater.readRemoteManifest();
```

```
      const

needsUpdate = await updater.checkNewVersion( rManifest );
    if ( !needsUpdate ) {
      return;
    }


    if ( !confirm( "New release is available. Do you want to upgrade?" ) )
{
      return;
    }



    // Subscribe for progress events
    updater.on( "download", ( downloadSize, totalSize ) => {

 const procent = Math.floor( downloadSize / totalSize * 100 );
      el.innerHTML = `Downloading - ${procent}%`;
    });
    updater.on( "install", ( installFiles, totalFiles ) => {
      const procent = Math.floor(

installFiles / totalFiles * 100 );
      el.innerHTML = `Installing - ${procent}%`;
    });


const updateFile = await updater.download( rManifest );
    await updater.unpack( updateFile );


await updater.restartToSwap();
  } catch ( e ) {
    console.error( e );
  }
}

exports.start = start;
```

Here, we applied the async/await syntax of ES2016. By prefixing the function with `async`, we state that it is asynchronous. After that, we can use await in front of any Promise (`https://mzl.la/1jLTOHB`) to receive its resolved value. If Promise rejects it, the exception will be caught in the try/catch statement.

What exactly does the code do? As we agreed, it compares local and remote manifest versions.

If release server has the newer version, it informs the user using the JavaScript confirm function. If the user is positive on upgrading, it downloads the latest release and unpacks it. While downloading and unpacking, the updater object emits the corresponding messages; so, we can subscribe and represent the progress. When ready, the service restarts the application for swapping; so, now it replaces the outdated version with the downloaded one and restarts again. On the way, the service reports to the user by writing in the passed-in HTML element (el). By the design it expects the element representing the path container in the title bar.

So, we can now enable the service in the main module:

`./client/js/app.js`

```
const { start } = require( "./js/Service/Autoupdate" ),
// start autoupdate
setTimeout(() => {

start( document.querySelector( "[data-bind=path]" ) );
}, 500 );
```

Well, how do we test it? We jump to client folder and build a distribution package:

```
npm run package
```

Supposedly, it lands in server/releases. We unpack to the arbitrary location, for example, `~/sandbox/`:

```
unzip ../server/releases/file-explorer-linux-x64.zip -d ~/sandbox/
```

Here, we will find the executable (for Linux, it will be `file-explorer`) and run it. The File Explorer will work as usual because the release server doesn't have a newer version, so we go back to the client folder and create one:

```
npm version patch
```

Now we switch to the server folder and edit the version of the manifest to match the just-generated one (1.0.1).

Then, we restart the bundled app (for example, `~/sandbox/file-explorer`) and observe the prompt:

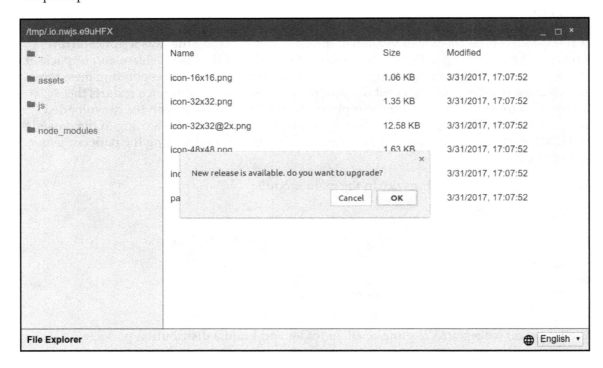

After clicking on **OK**, we see the progress on downloading and installing in the title bar:

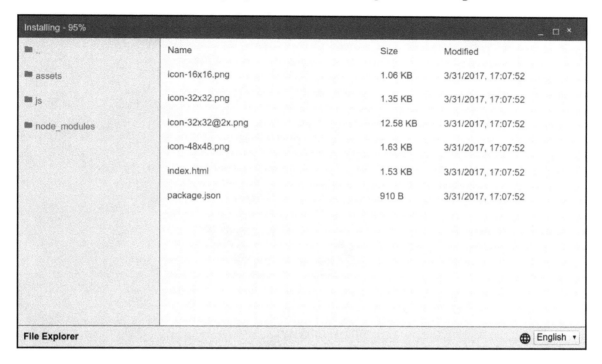

Then, the application restarts and reports swapping. When done, it restarts again, now updated.

Summary

In the beginning of this chapter, our File Explorer could only navigate the filesystem and open files. We extended it to show a file in the folder, and to copy/paste and delete files. We exploited the NW.js API to provide the files with the dynamically-built context menu. We learned to exchange text and images between applications using system clipboard. We made our File Explorer support diverse command-line options. We provided support for internalization and localization, and examined the protection of the sources through compilation in the native code. We went through the packaging process and prepared for distribution. Finally, we set up a release server and extended the File Explorer with a service for autoupdating.

3

Creating a Chat System with Electron and React – Planning, Designing, and Development

In the previous chapters, we worked with NW.js. It's a great framework, but not the only one on the market. Its counterpart Electron isn't inferior to NW.js in feature set and has an even larger community. To make the right choice of what fits best, I assume that one has to try both frameworks. So, our next example application will be a simple chat system and we will do it with Electron. We made the file explorer in plain JavaScript. We had to take care of abstractions consistency, data binding, templating, and such. In fact, we can delegate these tasks to a JavaScript framework. At the time of writing, the three solutions--React, Vue, and Angular--head the short list, where React seems like the most trending. I find it as a best fit for our next application. So, we will look into the essentials of React. We will set up Electron and webpack for our React-based application. We will not write all the CSS styles manually this time, but will use PhotonKit markup components. Finally, we will build the chat static prototype using React components and get ready to make it functional.

Application blueprint

In order to describe our application requirements, the same as previously, we start with user stories:

- As a user, I can introduce myself to the chat
- As a user, I can see real time the list of chat participants
- As a user, I can enter and submit a message
- As a user, I can see messages of chat participants as they are coming

If putting it onto wireframes, the first screen will be a simple prompt for a username:

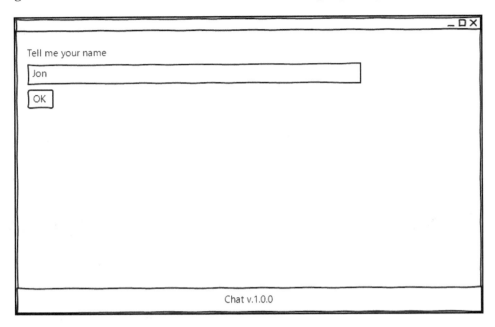

The second screen contains a sidebar with participants and the main area with the conversation thread and a form to submit a message:

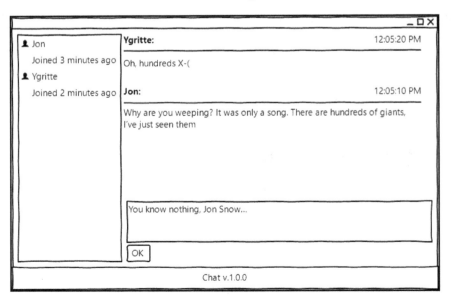

The second screen shares header and footer with the first one, but the main section consists of a participant list (on the left) and chat pane (on the right). The chat pane comprises incoming messages and submission form.

Electron

We have already become acquainted with NW.js. As you likely know, there is an alternative to it called Electron (`https://electron.atom.io/`). By and large, both provide comparable feature sets (`http://bit.ly/28NW0iX`). On the other hand, we can observe that Electron has a larger and much more active community (`https://electron.atom.io/community/`).

Electron is also known to be the GUI framework behind notable open source projects, such as Visual Studio Code (`https://code.visualstudio.com/`) and Atom IDE (`https://atom.io/`).

From a developer perspective, the first difference one faces is that Electron's entry point is a JavaScript, unlike HTML in NW.js. As we launch an Electron application, the framework runs first the specified script (main process). The script creates the application window. Electron provides API split in modules. Some of them are available only for the main process, some for renderer processes (any scripts requested from web pages originated by the main script).

Let's put this into practice. First of all, we will create the `./package.json` manifest file:

```
{
  "name": "chat",
  "version": "1.0.0",
  "main": "./app/main.js",
  "scripts": {
    "start": "electron ."
  },
  "devDependencies": {
    "devtron": "^1.4.0",
    "electron": "^1.6.2",
    "electron-debug": "^1.1.0"
  }
}
```

On the whole, this manifest doesn't differ much from the one we created in previous chapters for NW.js. Yet, we do not need the `window` field here and field `main` points at the main process script.

As for dependencies, we obviously need `electron`, and in addition, we will use the `electron-debug` package, which activates hotkeys *F12* and *F5* for DevTools and reload, respectively (`https://github.com/sindresorhus/electron-debug`). We also include Electron's DevTools Extension, called Devtron (`https://electron.atom.io/devtron`).

Now, we can edit the main process script:

`./app/main.js`

```
const { app, BrowserWindow } = require( "electron" ),
      path = require( "path" ),
      url = require( "url" );

let mainWindow;
```

Here, we import `app` and `BrowserWindow` from the `electron` module. The first one allows us to subscribe to application lifecycle events. With the second, we create and control the browser window. We also obtain references to NPM modules `path` and `url`. The first helps to create platform-agnostic paths and the second helps in building a valid URL. In the last line, we declare a global reference for the browser window instance. Next, we will add a function that creates the browser window:

```
function createWindow() {
  mainWindow = new BrowserWindow({
    width: 1000, height: 600
  });

  mainWindow.loadURL( url.format({
    pathname: path.join( __dirname, "index.html" ),
    protocol: "file:",
    slashes: true
  }) );

  mainWindow.on( "closed", () => {
    mainWindow = null;
  });
}
```

Actually, the function just creates a window instance and loads `index.html` in it. When the window is closed, the reference to the window instance gets destroyed. Further, we subscribe for application events:

```
app.on( "ready", createWindow );

app.on( "window-all-closed", () => {
  if ( process.platform !== "darwin" ) {
```

```
    app.quit();
  }
});

app.on( "activate", () => {
  if ( mainWindow === null ) {
    createWindow();
  }
});
```

The application event "`ready`" is fired when Electron finishes initialization; then we create the browser window.

The `window-all-closed` event is emitted when all the windows are closed. For any platform but macOS, we quit the application. OS X applications usually stay active until the user quit explicitly.

The `activate` event gets triggered only on macOS. In particular, it happens when we click on the application's dock or taskbar icon. If no window exists at that moment, we create a new one.

Finally, we call `electron-debug` to activate the debug hotkeys:

```
require( "electron-debug" )();
```

If we launch Electron now, it will try loading `index.html`, which we have to create first:

`./app/index.html`

```html
<!DOCTYPE html>
<html>
  <head>
    <meta charset="UTF-8">
    <title>Hello World!</title>
  </head>
  <body>
    <ul>
      <li id="app"></li>
      <li id="os"></li>
      <li id="electronVer"></li>
    </ul>
  </body>
  <script src="./renderer.js"></script>
</html>
```

Nothing exciting is happening here. We just declared several placeholders and loaded a renderer process script:

`./app/renderer.js`

```
const manifest = require( "../package.json" );

const platforms = {
  win32: "Windows",
  darwin: "macOS",
  linux: "Linux"
};

function write( id, text ){
  document.getElementById( id ).innerHTML = text;
}

write( "app", `${manifest.name} v.${manifest.version}` );
write( "os", `Platform: ${platforms[ process.platform ]}` );
write( "electronVer", `Electron v.${process.versions.electron}` );
```

In the renderer script, we read `package.json` into the `manifest` constant. We define a dictionary object to map the `process.platform` keys to meaningful platform names. We add a helper function, `write`, which assigns a given text to the element matching the given ID. Using this function, we populate the placeholders of the HTML.

At this point, we are expected to have the following file structure:

```
.
├── app
│   ├── index.html
│   ├── main.js
│   └── renderer.js
├── node_modules
└── package.json
```

Now, we install dependencies (`npm i`) and run the (`npm start`) example. We will see the following window:

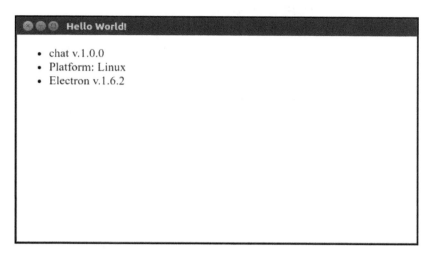

React

React is gaining momentum. It is the most trending technology, according to the 2016 Stack Overflow developer survey (`http://stackoverflow.com/insights/survey/2016#techno logy`). It is interesting to note that React is not even a framework. It's a JavaScript library for building user interfaces--very clean, concise, and powerful. The library implements the component-driven architecture. So, we create components (reusable, composable, and stateful units of UI) and then use them like Lego blocks to construct the intended UI. React treats the derived structure as an in-memory DOM representation (virtual DOM). As we bind it to the real DOM, React keeps both in sync, meaning that whenever any of its components change their states, React immediately reflects the view changes in the DOM.

 Besides that, we can convert virtual DOM in the HTML string (`http://bit.ly/2oVsjVn`) on the server side and send it with an HTTP response. The client side will automatically bind to the already existing HTML. Thus, we speed up page loading and allow search engines to crawl the content.

In a nutshell, the component is a function that takes in given properties and returns an element, where an element is a plain object representing a component or a DOM node. Alternatively, one can use a class extending React.Component, whose render method produces the element:

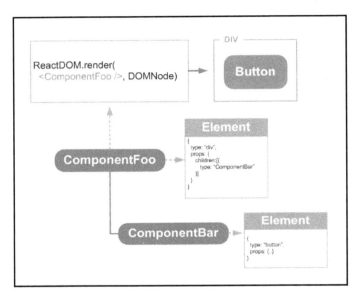

To create an Element, one can go with the API. Yet, nowadays, as a rule, it's not used directly, but via syntactic sugar known as **JSX**. JSX extends JavaScript with a new type that looks like an HTML template:

```
const name = "Jon", surname = "Snow";
const element = <header>
  <h1>{name + " " + surname}</h1>
</header>;
```

Basically, we write HTML straight in JavaScript and JavaScript in HTML. JSX can be translated to plain JavaScript using the Babel compiler with preset react (https://babeljs.io/docs/plugins/preset-react/).

Most of the modern IDEs support JSX syntax from the box.

To have a better understanding, we fiddle a bit with React. A function-based component might look like this:

```
function Header( props ){
  const { title } = props;
  return (
    <header>
      <h1>{title}</h1>
    </header>
  );
}
```

So, we declare a `Header` component that generates an element representing a header with a heading populated from the `title` property. We can also go with a class. Thus, we can encapsulate component-related methods in the class scope:

```
import React from "react";

class Button extends React.Component {
  onChange(){
    alert( "Clicked!" );
  }

  render() {
    const { text } = this.props;
    return <button onChange={this.onChange.bind( this )} >{text}</button>;
  }
}
```

This component creates a button and provides it with a minimalistic functionality (when the button is clicked, we get an alert box with the **Clicked!** text).

Now, we can attach our components to the DOM, as follows:

```
import ReactDOM from "react-dom";

ReactDOM.render(<div>
  <Header   />
  <Button text="Click me" />
</div>, document.querySelector( "#app" ) );
```

As you can note, components imply a unidirectional flow. You can pass properties from parent to child, but not otherwise. Properties are immutable. When we need to communicate from a child, we lift the state up:

```
import React from "react";

class Item extends React.Component {
  render(){
    const { onSelected, text } = this.props;
    return <li onClick={onSelected( text )}>{text}</li>;
  }
}

class List extends React.Component {

  onItemSelected( name ){
    // take care of ...
  }

  render(){
    const names = [ "Gregor Clegane", "Dunsen", "Polliver" ];
    return <nav>
        <ul>{names.map(( name ) => {
            return <Item name={name} onSelected={this.onItemSelected.bind(
this )} />;
          })}
        </ul>
      </nav>;
  }
}
```

In the `render` method of the `List` component, we have an array of names. Using the `map` array prototype method, we iterate through the name list. The method results in an array of elements, which JSX accepts gladly. While declaring `Item`, we pass in the current `name` and `onItemSelected` handler bound to the list instance scope. The `Item` component renders `<li>` and subscribes the passed-in handler to click events. Therefore, events of a child component are handled by the parent.

Electron meets React

Now, we have an idea about both Electron and React. What about on how to use them together? To get a grasp on it, we will start not with our real application, but with a simple, similar example. It will include a few components and a form. The application will reflect user input in the window title. I suggest cloning our last example. We can reuse the manifest and main process script. However we have to bring the following changes to the manifest:

`./package.json`

```
{
  "name": "chat",
  "version": "1.0.0",
  "main": "./app/main.js",
  "scripts": {
    "start": "electron .",
    "dev": "webpack -d --watch",
    "build": "webpack"
  },
  "dependencies": {
    "prop-types": "^15.5.7",
    "react": "^15.4.2",
    "react-dom": "^15.4.2"
  },
  "devDependencies": {
    "babel-core": "^6.22.1",
    "babel-loader": "^6.2.10",
    "babel-plugin-transform-class-properties": "^6.23.0",
    "babel-preset-es2017": "^6.22.0",
    "babel-preset-react": "^6.22.0",
    "devtron": "^1.4.0",
    "electron": "^1.6.2",
    "electron-debug": "^1.1.0",
    "webpack": "^2.2.1"
  }
}
```

In the preceding example, we add the react and react-dom modules. The first is the library core and the second serves as a glue between React and DOM. The prop-types module brings us type-checking abilities (till React v.15.5, which was a built-in object of the library). We add webpack as a dev-dependency in addition to electron-specific modules. Webpack is a module bundler that takes in varying types (sources, images, markup, and CSS) of assets and produces a bundle(s) that can be loaded by the client. We will use webpack to bundle our React/JSX-based application.

However, webpack doesn't transpile JSX its own; it uses the Babel compiler (`babel-core`). We also include the `babel-loader` module, which bridges between webpack and Babel. The `babel-preset-react` module is a so-called Babel preset (a set of plugins) that allows Babel to deal with JSX. With the `babel-preset-es2017` preset, we make Babel compile our ES2017-compliant code into ES2016, which is greatly supported by Electron. What is more, I included the `babel-plugin-transform-class-properties` Babel plugin to unlock features of the proposal called ES Class Fields & Static Properties (`https://github.com/tc39/proposal-class-public-fields`). So, we will be able to define class properties directly without the help of a constructor, which did not yet land to the specification.

There are two extra commands in the scripts section. The `build` command bundles JavaScript for the client. The `dev` command sets webpack in a watch mode. So, whenever we change any of the sources, it automatically bundles the application.

Before using webpack, we will need to configure it:

`./webpack.config.js`

```
const { join } = require( "path" ),
      webpack = require( "webpack" );

module.exports = {
  entry: join( __dirname, "app/renderer.jsx" ),
  target: "electron-renderer",
  output: {
      path: join( __dirname, "app/build" ),
      filename: "renderer.js"
  },
  module: {
    rules: [
      {
        test: /.jsx?$/,
        exclude: /node_modules/,
        use: [{
          loader: "babel-loader",
          options: {
            presets: [ "es2017", "react" ],
            plugins: [ "transform-class-properties" ]
          }
        }]
      }
    ]
  }
};
```

We set `app/renderer.jsx` as the entry point. So, webpack will read it first and resolve any met dependencies recursively. The compiled bundle can be found then in `app/build/renderer.js`. So far, we have set the only rule for webpack: every met `.js` or `.jsx` file with the exception of the `node_modules` directory goes to Babel, which is configured for the `es2017` and `react` presets (and the `transform-class-properties` plugin, to be precise). So, if we run now, the `npm run build` webpack will try compiling `app/renderer.jsx` into `app/build/renderer.js`, which we call from the HTML.

The code for the `./app/index.html` file is as follows:

```html
<!DOCTYPE html>
<html>
  <head>
    <meta charset="UTF-8">
    <title>Hello World!</title>
  </head>
  <body>
    <app></app>
  </body>
  <script>
   require( "./build/renderer.js" );
  </script>
</html>
```

The main renderer script may look as follows:

`./app/renderer.jsx`

```jsx
import React from "react";
import ReactDOM from "react-dom";

import Header from "./Components/Header.jsx";
import Copycat from "./Components/Copycat.jsx";

ReactDOM.render((
<div>
  <Header />
  <Copycat>
    <li>Child node</li>
    <li>Child node</li>
  </Copycat>
</div>
), document.querySelector( "app" ) );
```

Here, we import two components--`Header` and `Copycat`--and use them in a composite one, which we bind to the DOM custom element, `<app>`.

The following is the first component we describe with a function:

`./app/Components/Header.jsx`

```
import React from "react";
import PropTypes from "prop-types";

export default function Header( props ){
  const { title } = props;
  return (
    <header>
      <h3>{title}</h3>
    </header>
  );
}

Header.propTypes = {
  title: PropTypes.string
};
```

The function in the preceding code takes one property--`title` (we passed it in the parent component, `<Header />`)--and renders it as a heading.

Note that we use `PropTypes` to validate the `title` property value. If we happen to set a value other than string to `title`, a warning will be shown in the JavaScript console.

The following second component is presented with a class:

`./app/Components/Copycat.jsx`

```
import React from "react";
import { remote } from "electron";

export default class Copycat extends React.Component {

  onChange( e ){
    remote.getCurrentWindow().setTitle( e.target.value );
  }

  render() {
    return (
      <div>
        <input placeholder="Start typing here"
onChange={this.onChange.bind( this )} />
```

```
          <ul>
          {this.props.children}
          </ul>
        </div>
      )
    }
}
```

This component renders an input field. Whatever one is typing in the field gets reflected in the window title. Here, I have set a goal to show a new concept: children components/nodes.

Do you remember we declared `Copycat` with children nodes in the parent component? The code for the `Copycat` element is as follows:

```
<Copycat>
    <li>Child node</li>
    <li>Child node</li>
</Copycat>
```

Now, we receive these list items in `this.props.children` and render them within `<ul>`.

Besides this, we subscribe a `this.onChange` handler for change events on the input element. As it changes, we obtain a current window instance from the remote function of electron (`remote.getCurrentWindow()`) and replace its title with input contents.

To see what we've got, we install dependencies using `npm i`, build the project using `npm run build`, and launch the application using `npm start`:

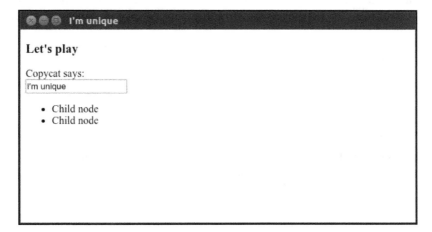

Enabling DevTools extensions

I believe that you had no problems when running the last example. Yet, when we need to trace an issue in a React application, it can be tricky, as DevTools shows us what is happening to the real DOM; however, we want to know about the virtual one also. Fortunately, Facebook offers an extension for DevTools called React Developer Tools (http://bit.ly/1dGLkxb).

We will install this extension with electron-devtools-installer (https://www.npmjs.com/package/electron-devtools-installer). This tool supports a number of DevTools extensions including a few React-related: React Developer Tools (REACT_DEVELOPER_TOOLS), Redux DevTools Extension (REDUX_DEVTOOLS), React Perf (REACT_PERF). We will pick only the first one for now.

First we install the package:

```
npm i -D electron-devtools-installer
```

Then we add to the main process script the following line:

./app/main.js

```
const { default: installExtension, REACT_DEVELOPER_TOOLS } = require(
"electron-devtools-installer" );
```

We imported from the package installExtension function and REACT_DEVELOPER_TOOLS constant, which represents **React Developer Tools** . Now we can call the function as soon as application is ready. On this event we already invoke our createWindow function. So we can extend the function rather than subscribe again for the event:

```
function createWindow() {
    installExtension(REACT_DEVELOPER_TOOLS)
        .then((name) => console.log(`Added Extension: ${name}`))
        .catch((err) => console.log("An error occurred: ", err));
//..
```

Now, when I launch the application and open DevTools (*F12*), I can see a new tab, React, which brings me to the corresponding panel. Now, it is possible to navigate through the React component tree, select its nodes, and inspect the corresponding components, edit its props, and state:

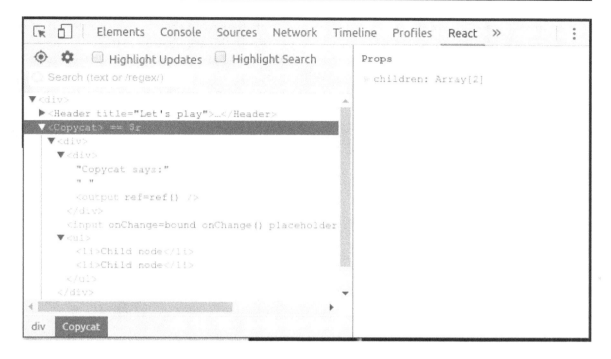

Static prototype

At this point, we are quite ready to start with the chat application. Yet, it will be easier to grasp if we create first a static version and then extend it with the intended functionality. Nowadays, developers often do not write CSS from scratch, but reuse components of HTML/CSS frameworks such as Bootstrap. There is a framework dedicated for the Electron application--**Photonkit** (http://photonkit.com). This framework provides us with building blocks such as layouts, panes, sidebar, lists, buttons, forms, table, and buttons. A UI constructed of these blocks looks in the style of macOS, automatically adapted for Electron and responsive to its viewport size. Ideally, I would go with ready PhotonKit components built with React (http://react-photonkit.github.io), but we will do it with HTML. I want to show you how you can incorporate an arbitrary third-party CSS framework on the example of PhotonKit.

First, we install it with NPM:

```
npm i -S photonkit
```

What we really need from the package is CSS and fonts files from the `dist` subfolder. The only truly reliable way to access the package content from the application is the require function (`http://bit.ly/2oGu0Vn`). It's clear how to request JavaScript or JSON files, but what about other types, for example, CSS? With webpack, we can bundle theoretically any content. We just need to specify the corresponding loaders in the webpack configuration file:

`./webpack.config.js`

```
...
module.exports = {
{
 ...
 module: {
    rules: [
      ...
      {
        test: /\.css$/,
        use: ["style-loader", "css-loader"]
      }
    ]
  }
};
```

We extended webpack configuration with a new rule that matches any files with extension `css`. Webpack will process such files with `style-loader` and `css-loader`. The first one reads the requested file and adds it to the DOM by injecting a style block. The second brings to the DOM any assets requested with `@import` and `url()`.

After enabling this rule, we can load Photon styles directly in a JavaScript module:

```
import "photonkit/dist/css/photon.css";
```

However, the custom fonts used in this CSS still won't be available. We can fix it by further extending the webpack configuration:

`./webpack.config.js`

```
module.exports = {
  ...
  module: {
    rules: [
      ...
      {
        test: /\.(eot|svg|ttf|woff|woff2)(\?v=[0-9]\.[0-9]\.[0-9])?$/,
        use: [{
            loader: "file-loader",
```

```
        options: {
          publicPath: "./build/"
        }
      }]
    }
  ]
}
};
```

This rule aims for font files and exploits `file-loader`, which takes the requested file from the package, stores it locally, and returns the newly created local path.

So, given that the styles and fonts are handled by webpack, we can proceed with components. We will have two components representing the window header and footer. For the main section, we will use `Welcome` when the user has not yet provided any name, and `ChatPane` afterward. The second one is a layout for `Participants` and `Conversation` components. We will also have a root component, `App`, that connects all other components with the future chat services. Actually, this one works not like a presentational component, but as a container (`http://redux.js.org/docs/basics/UsageW ithReact.html`). So, we are going to keep it separate from others.

As we are now done with the architecture, we can write down our start script:

`./app/renderer.jsx`

```
import "photonkit/dist/css/photon.css";
import React from "react";
import ReactDOM from "react-dom";

import App from "./Containers/App.jsx";

ReactDOM.render((
<App />
), document.querySelector( "app" ) );
```

Here, we add to the DOM the CSS of PhotonKit library (`import "photonkit/dist/css/photon.css"`) and bind the `App` container to the `<app>` element. The following container goes next:

`./app/js/Containers/App.jsx`

```
import React from "react";
import PropTypes from "prop-types";
import ChatPane from "../Components/ChatPane.jsx";
import Welcome from "../Components/Welcome.jsx";
import Header from "../Components/Header.jsx";
```

```
import Footer from "../Components/Footer.jsx";

export default class App extends React.Component {

  render() {
    const name = "Name";
    return (
      <div className="window">
        <Header></Header>
        <div className="window-content">
          { name ?
            ( <ChatPane
                /> ) :
            ( <Welcome /> ) }
        </div>
        <Footer></Footer>
      </div>
    );
  }
}
```

At this stage, we just lay out other components using PhotonKit application layout styles (`.window` and `.window-content`). As we have agreed, we render either `ChatPane` or `Welcome` between header and footer, depending on the value of the local constant, `name`.

By the way, both the header and footer we build from Photon mark-up component (`http://photonkit.com/components/`) are called **bar**. Besides a neat styling, it also enables the possibility to drag the application window around your desktop:

`./app/js/Components/Header.jsx`

```
import React from "react";

export default class Header extends React.Component {
  render() {
    return (
      <header className="toolbar toolbar-header">
          <div className="toolbar-actions">
              <button className="btn btn-default pull-right">
                  <span className="icon icon-cancel"></span>
              </button>
          </div>
      </header>
    )
  }
}
```

As you can figure out from Photon CSS classes in the `Header` component (`.toolbar` and `.toolbar-header`), we render a bar on the top of the window. The bar accepts action buttons (`.toolbar-actions`). At the moment, the only button available is meant to close the window.

In the `Footer` component, we render a bar positioned at the bottom (`.toolbar-footer`):

`./app/js/Components/Footer.jsx`

```
import React from "react";
import * as manifest from "../../../package.json";

export default function Footer(){
    return (
      <footer className="toolbar toolbar-footer">
        <h1 className="title">{manifest.name} v.{manifest.version}</h1>
      </footer>
    );
}
```

It includes the project name and version from the manifest.

For the welcome screen, we a have a simple form with the input field (`input.form-control`) for the name and a submit button (`button.btn-primary`):

`./app/js/Components/Welcome.jsx`

```
import React from "react";

export default class Welcome extends React.Component {

  render() {
    return (
      <div className="pane padded-more">
        <form>
          <div className="form-group">
            <label>Tell me your name</label>
            <input required className="form-control" placeholder="Name"
          />
          </div>
          <div className="form-actions">
            <button className="btn btn-form btn-primary">OK</button>
          </div>
        </form>
      </div>
    )
  }
```

```
}
```

The `ChatPane` component places `Participants` on the left and `Conversation` on the right. It's pretty much everything what it does at the moment:

`./app/js/Components/ChatPane.jsx`

```
import React from "react";

import Participants from "./Participants.jsx";
import Conversation from "./Conversation.jsx";

export default function ChatPane( props ){
  return (
    <div className="pane-group">
      <Participants />
      <Conversation />
    </div>
  );

}
```

In the `Participants` component, we use a layout pane of a type sidebar (`.pane.pane-sm.sidebar`):

`./app/js/Components/Participants.jsx`

```
import React from "react";

export default class Participants extends React.Component {
  render(){
    return (
      <div className="pane pane-sm sidebar">
        <ul className="list-group">
          <li className="list-group-item">
            <div className="media-body">
              <strong><span className="icon icon-
user"></span> Name</strong>
              <p>Joined 2 min ago</p>
            </div>
          </li>
        </ul>
      </div>
    );
  }
}
```

It has a list of chat participants. Every name we prefix with the Entype icon is provided by Photon.

The last component--Conversation--renders chat messages in a list (.list-group) and the submission form:

./app/js/Components/Conversation.jsx

```jsx
import React from "react";

export default class Conversation extends React.Component {

    render(){
        return (
            <div className="pane padded-more l-chat">
                <ul className="list-group l-chat-conversation">
                    <li className="list-group-item">
                        <div className="media-body">
                            <time className="media-body__time">10.10.2010</time>
                            <strong>Name:</strong>
                                <p>Text...</p>
                        </div>
                    </li>
                </ul>
                <form className="l-chat-form">
                    <div className="form-group">
                        <textarea required placeholder="Say something..."
                            className="form-control"></textarea>
                    </div>
                    <div className="form-actions">
                        <button className="btn btn-form btn-primary">OK</button>
                    </div>
                </form>
            </div>
        );
    }
}
```

This is the first time we need to have a few custom styles:

./app/assets/css/custom.css

```css
.l-chat {
    display: flex;
    flex-flow: column nowrap;
    align-items: stretch;
}
.l-chat-conversation {
    flex: 1 1 auto;
    overflow-y: auto;
}
.l-chat-form {
    flex: 0 0 110px;
```

```
  }
.media-body__time {
  float: right;
}
```

Here, we make the form (.l-form) stick to the bottom. It has a fixed height (110px), and all the available space upward takes the message list (.l-chat-conversation). In addition, we align message time information (.media-body__time) to the right and take it out of the flow (float: right).

This CSS can be loaded in HTML:

./index.html

```html
<!DOCTYPE html>
<html>
  <head>
    <meta charset="UTF-8">
    <title>Chat</title>
    <link href="./assets/css/custom.css" rel="stylesheet" type="text/css"/>
  </head>
  <body>
    <app></app>
  </body>
  <script>
   require( "./build/renderer.js" );
  </script>
</html>
```

We make sure that all the dependencies are installed (npm i), then build (npm run build) and launch the application (npm start). As it's done, we can see the following intended UI:

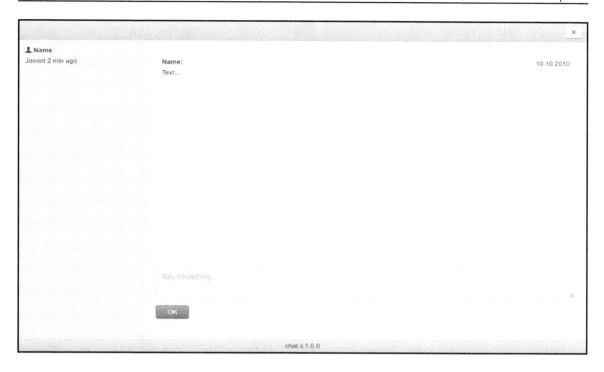

Summary

Despite the fact that we do not have a functional application yet and just a static prototype, we have come a long way. We talked about the Electron GUI framework. We compared it to NW.js and went through its peculiarities. We made a simplified Electron demo application consisting of a main process script, renderer one, and HTML. We had an introduction into React basics. We focused on components and elements, JSX and virtual DOM, props, and state. We configured webpack to compile our ES.Next-compliant JSX into a JavaScript-acceptable one by Electron. To consolidate our knowledge, we made a small demo React application powered by Electron. What is more, we examined how to enable a DevTools extension (React Developer Tools) in Electron to trace and debug React applications. We have briefly familiarized ourselves with the PhotonKit frontend framework and created React components for the chat application using PhotonKit styles and markup. Finally, we have bundled our components together and rendered the application in Electron.

4
Creating a Chat System with Electron and React – Enhancement, Testing, and Delivery

We finished the last chapter with a static prototype. We learned about React, composed the components, but didn't provide them with any state. Now, we will start binding the state of the application window to the Header component. As the state concept clarified, we will move to the chat services. After getting a brief introduction to the WebSockets technology, we will implement both the server and client. We will bind the service events to the application state. Finally, we will have a fully working chat. We won't stop on it, but will take care of the technical debt. So, we will set up the Jest testing framework and unit-test both the stateless and stateful components. Afterward, we will package the application and publish releases though a basic HTTP server. We will extend the application to update when new releases are available.

Revitalizing the title bar

Until now, our title bar was not really useful. Thanks to the Photon framework, we can already use it as a handle to drag and drop the window across the viewport, yet we are missing windowing actions such as close, maximize, and restore window.

Let's implement them:

`./app/js/Components/Header.jsx`

```
import { remote } from "electron";
const win = remote.getCurrentWindow();

export default class

Header extends React.Component {
//....
 onRestore = () => {
    win.restore();
  }
  onMaximize = () => {
    win.maximize();
  }
  onClose = () => {
    win.close();


  }
//...
 }
```

We do not go with methods, with properties keeping anonymous functions bound to the object scope. This trick is possible, thanks to `babel-plugin-transform-class-properties`, which we included in the manifest and Webpack configuration in Chapter 3, *Creating a Chat System with Electron and React – Planning, Design, and Development*.

We extended the component with handlers to close the window, to maximize, and then to restore to its original size. We already have a `close` button in JSX, so we just need to subscribe to the corresponding handler method for the `click` event using the `onClick` attribute:

```
<button className="btn btn-default pull-right" onClick={this.onClose}>
    <span className="icon

icon-cancel"></span>
</button>
```

The `maximize` and `restore` buttons, though, are rendered in HTML conditionally, depending on the current window state. Since we will utilize the state, let's define it:

```
constructor( props ) {
    super( props );
```

```
        this.state = { isMaximized: win.isMaximized() };
    }
```

The `isMaximized` state property takes in the corresponding flag from the current window instance. Now, we can extract this value from the state in JSX:

```
.....
render() {
    const { isMaximized } = this.state;
    return (
      <header

className="toolbar toolbar-header">
          <div className="toolbar-actions">

<button className="btn btn-default pull-right" onClick={this.onClose}>
                    <span

className="icon icon-cancel"></span>
                </button>

                {

isMaximized ? (
                    <button className="btn btn-default pull-right"
onClick={this.onRestore}>
                        <span className="icon icon-resize-small"></span>
                    </button> )

: (
                    <button className="btn btn-default pull-right"
onClick={this.onMaximize}>

        <span className="icon icon-resize-full"></span>
                    </button>)

    }

          </div>
      </header>
    )
}
```

So, we render the `restore` button when it is true and `maximize` otherwise. We also subscribe the handlers for the `click` events on both the buttons, but what about changing the state after the window maximizes or restores?

We can subscribe to the corresponding window events straight before the component is rendered to the DOM:

```
componentWillMount() {
    win.on( "maximize", this.updateState );
    win.on( "unmaximize",

this.updateState );
  }

  updateState = () => {
    this.setState({
      isMaximized:

win.isMaximized()
    });
  }
```

When the window changes its state handler, `updateState` invokes and actualizes the component state.

Utilizing WebSockets

We have a static prototype, and now we will make it functional. Any chat requires communication between connected clients. Usually, clients do not connect directly but through a server. The server registers connections and forwards the messages. It's pretty clear how to send a message from the client to server, but can we do it in the opposite direction? In the olden days, we had to deal with long-polling techniques. That worked, but with the overhead of HTTP, it is not really suitable when we mean a low latency application. Luckily for us, Electron supports WebSockets. With that API, we can open a full-duplex, bi-directional TCP connection between the client and server. WebSockets provides higher speed and efficiency as compared to HTTP. The technology brings reduction of upto 500:1 in unnecessary HTTP traffic and 3:1 in latency (`http://bit.ly/2ptVz1k`). You can find out more about WebSockets in my book *JavaScript Unlocked* (`https://www.packtpub.com/web-development/javascript-unlocked`). Here, we will get acquainted with the technology briefly, with the help of a small demo. I suggest examining an echo server and a client. Whenever a client sends a text to the server, the server broadcasts it on all the connected clients. So, on every page with the client loaded, we receive the message in real time.

Of course, we won't write a protocol implementation for the server, but go with an existing NPM package--nodejs-websocket (`https://www.npmjs.com/package/nodejs- websocket`):

```
npm i -S nodejs-websocket
```

Using the package API, we can quickly make our code to serve incoming messages from the client:

`./server.js`

```
const ws = require( "nodejs-websocket" ),
      HOST = "127.0.0.1",
      PORT = 8001;

const

server = ws.createServer(( conn ) => {

  conn.on( "text", ( text ) => {

server.connections.forEach( conn => {
      conn.sendText( text );
    });
  });


  conn.on( "error", ( err ) => {
    console.error( "Server error", err );
  });

});

server.listen( PORT, HOST, () => {
  console.info( "Server is ready" );
});
```

Here, we instantiate an object representing the WebSockets server (`server`). Within the callback of the `createServer` factory, we will receive connection objects. We subscribe to every connection for the "`text`" and "`error`" events. The first one happens when a data frame is sent from the client to the server. We simply forward it to every available connection. The second event is fired when something goes wrong, so we report the error. Finally, we start the server in the given port and host, for example, I set port `8001`. If this port is taken in your environment by any other program, just change the value of the `PORT` constant.

We can compose the client of this simplified chat as a single page application. So create the following HTML:

`./index.html`

```html
<!DOCTYPE html>
<html>
  <head>
    <title>Echo</title>

<meta charset="UTF-8">
    <meta name="viewport" content="width=device-width, initial-
    scale=1.0">

</head>
  <body>
    <form id="form">
      <input id="input" placeholder="Enter you

message..." />
      <button>Submit</button>
    </form>
    <output

id="output"></output>

<script>
const HOST = "127.0.0.1",
      PORT = 8001,

    form = document.getElementById( "form" ),
      input = document.getElementById( "input" ),
      output =

document.getElementById( "output" );

const ws = new WebSocket( `ws://${HOST}:${PORT}` );

ws.addEventListener( "error", ( e ) => {
  console.error( "Client's error: ", e );
});

ws.addEventListener( "open", () => {
  console.log( "Client connected" );
});

ws.addEventListener( "message", e => {
  output.innerHTML = e.data + "<br \>" + output.innerHTML;
```

```
});

form.addEventListener( "submit", ( e ) => {
  e.preventDefault();
  ws.send( input.value

);
});

</script>
  </body>
</html>
```

In the HTML, we placed a form with input control and output container. The intent is to send input value on form, submit it to the server, and display the server response in the output element.

In the JavaScript, we store a reference to the acting nodes and create an instance of the WebSockets client. We subscribe for the error, open, and message client events. The first two basically report on what is happening. The last one receives events from the server. In our case, the server sends text messages, so we can take them as e.data. We also need to handle the input from the client. Therefore, we subscribe for submit on the form element. We use the send method of the WebSockets client to dispatch the input value to the server.

To run the example, we can use the http-server module (https://www.npmjs.com/package/http-server) to launch a static HTTP server for our index.html:

npm i -S http-server

Now, we can add the following commands to package.json:

```
{
  "scripts": {
    "start:client": "http-server . -o",
    "start:server": "node server.js"
  }


}
```

So, we can run the server as:

npm run start:server

and then the client as:

```
npm run start:client
```

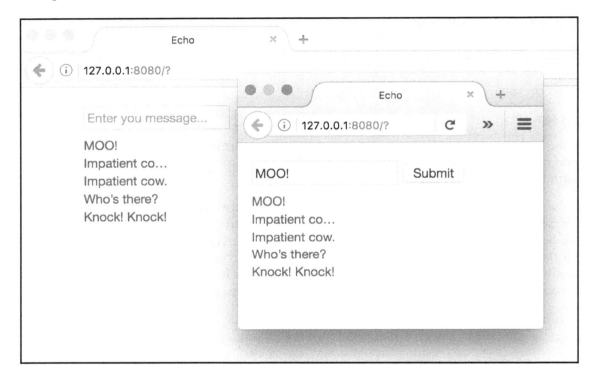

Implementing chat services

I believe that it's more or less clear how WebSockets works now, and we can apply the API for our chat. However, in a real application, we need something more than to echo sent texts. Let's put the intended event scenarios on paper:

- The `Welcome` component handles user input and sends via the client to the `join` server event with the entered user name in the payload
- The server receives the `join` event, adds a new user to the set, and broadcasts the `participants` event with the updated set
- The client receives the `participants` event and passes the set to the `Participants` component, which updates the participant's list

- The Conversation component handles user input and sends the entered message via the client to the server as the text event with username, text, and timestamp in the payload
- The server receives the text event and broadcasts it to all the chat participants

As we deal with event messages, we need a unified format for sending and receiving a single source of truth. So, we implement a message wrapper--`./app/js/Service/Message.js`:

```
class Message {
  static toString( event, data ){
    return JSON.stringify({
      event, data
    });
  }
  static fromString( text ){
    return JSON.parse( text );
  }
}

exports.Message = Message;
```

This module exposes two static methods. One transforms the given event name and payload into a JSON string, which can be sent through WebSockets; another translates the received string into a message object.

Now we write the server--`./app/js/Service/Server.js`:

```
import * as ws from "nodejs-websocket";
import { Message } from "./Message";

export default class

Server {

  constructor() {
    this.server = ws.createServer(( conn ) => {

conn.on( "error", ( err ) => {
      console.error( "Server error", err );
    });
    conn.on(

"close", ( code, reason ) => {
      console.log( "Server closes a connection", code, reason );
    });
```

```
            conn.on( "connection", () => {
              console.info( "Server creates a new connection" );

  });
      });

    }
  broadcast( event, data ){
    const text = Message.toString(

event, data );
      this.server.connections.forEach( conn => {
        conn.sendText( text );
      });
    }

  connect( host, port ) {
      this.server.listen( port, host, () => {

console.info( "Server is ready" );           });
    }
  }
```

The same as the echo server, this one subscribes to connection events to report what is going on and exposes the `broadcast` and `connect` methods. To make it handle incoming messages, we extend the `createServer` callback:

```
constructor() {
    this.server = ws.createServer(( conn ) => {

      conn.on( "text",

( text ) => {
        const msg = Message.fromString( text ),
            method = `on${msg.event}`;
        if ( !this[ method ] ) {
          return;
        }
        this[ method ]( msg.data, conn );

      });
      //...
    });
    //...
  }
```

Now, when receiving a message, the server tries to call a handler method matching the event name. For example, when it receives `join` event, it calls `onjoin`:

```
onjoin( name, conn ){
    const datetime = new Date();
    this.participants.set( conn, {

name: name,
        time: datetime.toString()
    });

    this.broadcast( "participants",

Array.from( this.participants.values() ));
    }
```

The method accepts the event payload (the user name here) as the first parameter and the connection reference as the second. It registers the connection in `this.participant` map. So, we can now determine the associated user name and registration timestamp by a connection. The method then broadcasts the values of the map as an array (a set of usernames and timestamps).

However, we shall not forget to define `this.participants` as a map in the class constructor:

```
constructor() {
    this.participants = new Map();
    //...
}
```

We also add a handler method for the `text` event:

```
ontext( data, conn ){
    const name = this.participants.get( conn ).name;
    this.broadcast(

"text", { name, ...data } );
    }
```

The method extracts the username associated with the given connection from the `this.participants`, extends the message payload with it, and broadcasts the derived message.

Now, we can write the client-- `./app/js/Service/Client.js`:

```
const EventEmitter = require( "events" ),
        READY_STATE_OPEN = 1;
import { Message } from

"./Message";


export default class Client extends EventEmitter {

  connect( host, port ){


    return new Promise(( resolve, reject ) => {
      this.socket = new WebSocket( `ws://${host}:${port}` );


      this.socket.addEventListener( "open", () => {
        resolve();
      });


      this.socket.addEventListener( "error", ( e ) => {
        if ( e.target.readyState > READY_STATE_OPEN ) {


          reject();
        }
      });

      this.socket.addEventListener( "message", e

=> {
        const msg = Message.fromString( e.data ),
            method = `on${msg.event}`;

 if ( !this[ method ] ) {
          return;
        }
        this[ method ]( msg.data );
      });


    });
  }
  onparticipants( data ){
```

```
      this.emit( "participants", data );
    }
    ontext( data ){
      this.emit( "text", data );
    }

  getParticipants(){

return this.participants;
    }
    join( userName ) {
      this.userName = userName;

this.send( "join", userName );
    }
    message( text ) {
      this.send( "text", {

userName: this.userName,
        text,
        dateTime: Date.now()
      });
    }
    send(

event, data ){
      this.socket.send( Message.toString( event, data ) );
    }
  }
```

The client implements the same trick with the handler methods as the server, but this time, we make the `connect` method return a Promise. Thus, we can adjust the execution flow if the client failed to connect the server. We have two handlers: `onparticipants` and `ontext`. Both of them simply bypass the received message to the application. Since the `Client` class extends `EventEmitter`, we can use `this.emit` to fire an event and any subscribed application module will be able to catch it. Besides, the client exposes two public methods: `join` and `message`. One (`join`) will be consumed by the `Welcome` component to register the provided username on the server, and the other (`message`) is called from the `Participants` component to communicate the submitted text to the server. Both the methods rely on the `send` private method, which actually dispatches messages.

Electron comprises of the Node.js runtime and therefore allows us to run the server. So, to make it simpler, we will include the server into the application. For that, we modify the server code again:

```
connect( host, port, client ) {
  client.connect( host, port ).catch(() => {

this.server.listen( port, host, () => {
    console.info( "Server is ready" );
    client.connect(

host, port ).catch(() => {
      console.error( "Client's error" );
    });
  });

});
  }
```

Now it runs the supplied `client.connect` to establish a connection with our WebSockets server. If it's the very first instance of the application running, no server is yet available. Therefore, the client fails to connect and execution flow jumps into the catch callback. There, we start the server and reconnect the client.

Bringing functionality to the components

Now when we have the server and client services, we can enable them in the application. The most suitable place is the `App` container--`./app/js/Containers/App.jsx`:

```
import Server from "../Service/Server";
import Client from "../Service/Client";

const HOST =

"127.0.0.1",
    PORT = 8001;

export default class App extends React.Component {

constructor(){
    super();
    this.client = new Client();
    this.server = new Server();
```

```
this.server.connect( HOST, PORT, this.client );
  }
//...
}
```

Do you remember that we rendered either the `ChatPane` or `Welcome` component conditionally in the static prototype?:

```
{ name ?
            ( <ChatPane client={client}
              /> ) :
            (

<Welcome  onNameChange={this.onNameChange} /> ) }
```

Back then, we hardcoded `name`, yet it belongs to the component state. So, we can initialize the state in the class constructor like this:

```
constructor(){
    //...
    this.state = {
      name: ""
    };
}
```

Well, `name` is empty by default and we, therefore, show the `Welcome` component. We can type in a new name there. As it's submitted, we need to somehow change the state in the parent component. We achieve it with a technique known as **Lifting state up**. We declare a handler for the `name` change event in the `App` container and pass it to the `Welcome` component with the props:

```
onNameChange = ( userName ) => {
  this.setState({ name: userName });
  this.client.join(

userName );
}

render() {
  const client = this.client,
        name = this.state.name;
  return (
    <div className="window">
      <Header></Header>
      <div
```

```
className="window-content">
        { name ?
          ( <ChatPane client={client}

/> ) :
            ( <Welcome  onNameChange={this.onNameChange} /> ) }
      </div>

<Footer></Footer>
    </div>
  );
}
```

So, we extract `name` from the state and use it in the expression. Initially, `name` is empty and therefore the `Welcome` component is rendered. We declare the `onNameChange` handler and pass it to the `Welcome` component with the props. The handler receives the submitted name, registers the new connection on the server (`this.client.join`), and changes the component state. So, the `ChatPane` component replaces `Welcome`.

Now, we will edit the `Welcome` component--`./app/js/Components/Welcome.jsx`:

```
import React from "react";
import PropTypes from "prop-types";

export default class Welcome extends

React.Component {

  onSubmit = ( e ) => {
    e.preventDefault();
    this.props.onNameChange(

this.nameEl.value || "Jon" );
  }

  static defaultProps = {
    onNameChange: () => {}

}

  static propTypes = {
    onNameChange: PropTypes.func.isRequired
  }

  render() {
```

```
      return (
        <div className="pane padded-more">
          <form onSubmit={this.onSubmit}>


            <div className="form-group">
              <label>Tell me your name</label>

          <input required className="form-control" placeholder="Name"
                ref={(input) => { this.nameEl

= input; }} />
            </div>
            <div className="form-actions">

<button className="btn btn-form btn-primary">OK</button>
            </div>

</form>
        </div>
      )
    }
  }
```

Whenever a component expects any props, it usually means that we have to apply the defaultProps and propTypes static methods. These belong to the React.Component API and are automatically called during component initialization. The first one sets a default value for the props and the second validates them. In HTML, we subscribe to the onSubmit handler for the form submit event. In the handler, we need to access an input value. With the ref JSX attribute, we added the instance as a reference to the input element. So, from the onSubmit handler, we can obtain the input value as this.nameEl.value.

Well, now the user can register in the chat, and we need to show the chat UI--
./app/js/Components/ChatPane.jsx:

```
export default function ChatPane( props ){
  const { client } = props;
  return (
    <div

className="pane-group">

      <Participants client={client} />

      <Conversation

client={client} />
```

```
        </div>
    );

}
```

This one is a composite component that lays out the `Participants` and `Conversation` children components and forwards `client` to them.

The first one is meant to display the list of participants--
`./app/js/Components/Participants.jsx`:

```
import React from "react";
import TimeAgo from "react-timeago";
import PropTypes from "prop-types";


export default class Participants extends React.Component {

 constructor( props ){
    super(
    props );
    this.state = {
      participants: props.client.getParticipants()
    }

props.client.on( "participants", this.onClientParticipants );
  }


  static defaultProps = {
    client: null
  }

  static propTypes = {
    client: PropTypes.object.isRequired
  }


 onClientParticipants = ( participants ) => {
    this.setState({
      participants:

participants
    })
  }
```

```
render(){
  return (
    <div className="pane pane-sm
    sidebar">
      <ul className="list-group">
        {this.state.participants.map(( user ) => (


          <li className="list-group-item" key={user.name}>
            <div className="media-
            body">
              <strong><span className="icon icon-user"></span> 
              {user.name}
              </strong>
              <p>Joined <TimeAgo date={user.time} /></p>
            </div>
          </li>
        ))}
      </ul>
    </div>
  );
}
}
```

Here, we need some construction work. First, we define the state, which includes the participant list from the props. We also subscribe to the client participants event and update the state every time the server sends an updated list. When rendering the list, we also show participant registration time, such as **joined 5 minutes ago**. For that, we use a third-party component, TimeAgo, provided by the react-timeago NPM package.

Eventually, we are coming to the Conversation component--
./app/js/Components/Conversation.jsx:

```
import React from "react";
import PropTypes from "prop-types";

export default class Conversation

extends React.Component {
  constructor( props ){
    super( props );
    this.messages = [];


    this.state = {
      messages: []
    }
```

```
      props.client.on( "text",  this.onClientText );
    }
    static defaultProps = {
      client: null
    }
    static propTypes = {
      client: PropTypes.object.isRequired
    }

onClientText = ( msg ) => {
    msg.time = new

Date( msg.dateTime );
    this.messages.unshift( msg );
    this.setState({
      messages: this.messages


    });
  }

  static normalizeTime( date, now, locale ){
    const isToday = (

now.toDateString() === date.toDateString() );
    // when local is undefined, toLocaleDateString/toLocaleTimeString

use default locale
    return isToday ? date.toLocaleTimeString( locale )
      : date.toLocaleDateString(

locale ) + ` ` + date.toLocaleTimeString( locale );
  }
  render(){
    const { messages } =

this.state;
    return (
        <div className="pane padded-more l-chat">
          <ul

className="list-group l-chat-conversation">
            {messages.map(( msg, i ) => (

<li className="list-group-item" key={i}>
                <div className="media-body">

    <time className="media-body__time">{Conversation.normalizeTime(
```

```
                 msg.time, new Date() )}</time>

              <strong>{msg.userName}:</strong>
                    {msg.text.split( "\n" ) .map(( line,
                    inx ) => (
                      <p key={inx}>{line}</p>
                    ))}
                </div>
                </li>
              ))}
          </ul>
        </div>
      );
    }
}
```

During the construction, we subscribe to the client `text` event and collect the received messages in the `this.messages` array. We use these messages to set the component state. In the `render` method, we extract the message list from the state and traverse it to render every item. The message view includes the sender's name, text, and time. The name we output as it is. We split the text in lines and wrap them with the paragraph element. To display time, we use the `normalizeTime` static method. This method transforms the `Date` object into a long string (date and time) when it's older than today, and into a short string (date) otherwise.

We also need a form for sending messages to the chat. The ideal method would be to put the form into a separate component, but for the sake of brevity, we will keep it next to the conversation view:

```
render(){
  const { messages } = this.state;
  return (
...
      <form onSubmit=

{this.onSubmit} className="l-chat-form">
          <div className="form-group">

<textarea required placeholder="Say something..."
          onKeyDown={this.onKeydown}

className="form-control" ref={ el => { this.inputEl = el; }}></textarea>
          </div>

          <div className="form-actions">
            <button className="btn btn-form btn-
```

```
primary">OK</button>
                </div>
            </form>
    );
}
...
```

Pretty much as in the `Welcome` component, we make a local reference to the text area node and subscribe the `onSubmit` handler for the form `submit` event. To make it user-friendly, we set `onKeydown` to listen to a keyboard event on the text area. When *Enter* is pressed during typing, we submit the form. So, we have to now add new handlers to the component class:

```
const ENTER_KEY = 13;
//...
onKeydown = ( e ) => {
    if ( e.which === ENTER_KEY && !

e.ctrlKey && !e.metaKey && !e.shiftKey ) {
        e.preventDefault();
        this.submit();
    }
  }
  onSubmit = ( e ) => {
    e.preventDefault();
    this.submit();

}

  submit() {
    this.props.client.message( this.inputEl.value );
    this.inputEl.value = "";


  }

//..
```

When the form is submitted either by pressing the **OK** button or *Enter*, we pass the message to the server via the `message` method of the client and reset the form.

I don't know about you, but I have the itch to run the application and see it in action. We have two options here. We can just start multiple instances from the same machine, register each one with a different name, and start chatting:

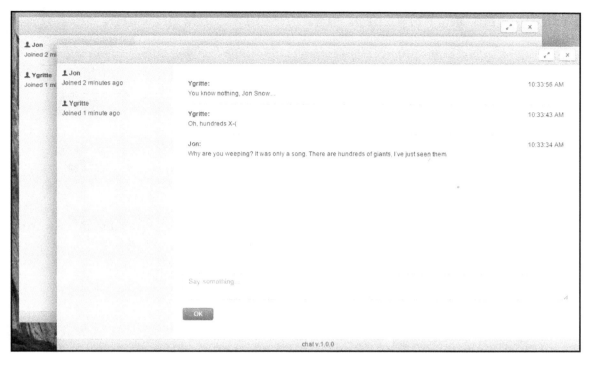

Alternatively, we set a public IP in the `App` container to make the chat available across the network.

Writing unit-tests

In real life, we cover application functionality with unit-tests. When it comes to React, the Jest testing framework is the first to pop up in one's mind. The framework is developed by Facebook as well as React. Jest is not aimed at React only; you can test any JavaScript. Just to see how it works, we can set up a new project:

```
npm init -y
```

Install Jest by running the following command:

```
npm i -D jest
```

Edit the `scripts` section in `package.json`:

```
"scripts": {
  "test": "jest"
}
```

Place the example unit for testing:

`./unit.js`

```
function double( x ){
  return x * 2;
}
exports.double = double;
```

This is a simple pure function that double any given number. What we need to do now is to just place a JavaScript file of a name matching the `*.(spec|test).js` pattern--
`./unit.spec.js`:

```
const { double } = require( "./unit" );
describe( "double", () => {
  it( "doubles a given number", () => {
    const x = 1;
    const res = double( x );
    expect( res ).toBe( 2 );
  });
});
```

If you are familiar with Mocha or, better, Jasmine, you will have no problem reading this test suite. We describe an aspect (`describe()`), declare our expectations (`it()`), and assert that the result produced by the unit under test meets the requirements (`expect()`). Basically, the syntax doesn't differ from the one we used in `Chapter 2`, *Creating a File Explorer with NW.js – Enhancement and Delivery*.

By running `npm test`, we get the following report:

```
PASS  ./unit.spec.js
  double
    ✓ doubles a given number (3ms)

Test Suites: 1 passed, 1 total
Tests:       1 passed, 1 total
Snapshots:   0 total
Time:        0.89s, estimated 1s
Ran all test suites.
```

What makes Jest preferable in our case is that it's really close to the React philosophy and incorporates specific features for testing a React application. For example, Jest comprises of the `toMatchSnapshot` assertion method. So, we can build a component in the virtual DOM, and make and save the snapshot of the element. Then, after refactoring, we run the tests. Jest takes actual snapshots of the modified components and compares them to the stored ones. That's a common approach for regression tests. Before putting it into practice, we have to set up Jest for our environment. We specified our bundling configuration in `webpack.config.js`. Jest won't consider this file. We have to compile the source for Jest separately, and we can do it with `babel-jest`:

```
npm i -D babel-jest
```

This plugin takes the code transformation instructions from the Babel runtime config--`./.babelrc`:

```
{
  "presets": [
    ["env", {
      "targets": { "node": 7 },
      "useBuiltIns": true
    }],
    "react"
  ],

  "plugins": [
    "transform-es2015-modules-commonjs",
  "transform-class-properties",
    "transform-object-rest-spread"
  ]
}
```

Here, we use preset env (`https://babeljs.io/docs/plugins/preset-env/`), which automatically determines and loads the plugins required by the target environment (Node.js 7). Do not forget to install the preset:

```
npm i -D babel-preset-env
```

We also apply the `transform-class-properties` and `transform-class-properties` plugins to get access to rest, spread, and ES Class Fields and Static Properties syntax, respectively (we have already used these plugins for Webpack configuration in Chapter 3, *Creating a Chat System with Electron and React – Planning, Design, and Development*).

As we did in the `normalizeTime` test example, we will modify the manifest--
`./package.json`:

```
{
  ...
    "scripts": {
      ...
      "test": "jest"
    },
    "jest": {

"roots": [
        "<rootDir>/app/js"
      ]
    },
  ...
}
```

This time, we also explicitly point Jest to our source directory, `app/js`.

As I explained earlier, we will produce snapshots of React components for further assertions. That can be achieved with the `react-test-renderer` package:

npm i -D react-test-renderer

Now we can write our first component regression test--
`./app/js/Components/Footer.spec.jsx`:

```
import * as React from "react";
import Footer from "./Footer";
import * as renderer from "react-test-

renderer";

describe( "Footer", () => {
  it( "matches previously saved snapshot", () => {

const tree = renderer.create(
      <Footer />
    );

    expect( tree.toJSON()

).toMatchSnapshot();
  });
});
```

Yeah, it turned out that easy. We create an element with `renderer.create` and obtain static data representation by calling the `toJSON` method. When we first run the test (`npm test`), it creates the __snapshots__ directory with the snapshot next to the test file. Every subsequent time, Jest compares the stored snapshots to the actual ones.

If you want to reset snapshots, just run `npm test -- -u`.

Testing a stateful component is similar--
`./app/js/Components/Participants.spec.jsx`:

```
import * as React from "react";
import Client from "../Service/Client";
import Participants from

"./Participants";
import * as renderer from "react-test-renderer";

describe( "Participants", () => {

  it( "matches previously saved snapshot", () => {
    const items = [{
        name: "Jon",
        time: new Date( 2012, 2, 12, 5, 5, 5, 5 ) }
      ],
      client = new Client(),

    component = renderer.create( <Participants client={client} />
    );

  component.getInstance

().onClientParticipants( items );
    expect( component.toJSON() ).toMatchSnapshot();
  });
});
```

We use the `getInstance` method of the created element to access the component instance. Thus, we can call the methods of the instance that set the concrete state. Here, we pass the fixture list of participants directly to the `onClientParticipants` handler. The component renders the list, and we make a snapshot.

Regression tests are good to check whether the component wasn't broken during refactoring, but they do not guarantee that the component behaved as intended in the first place. React provides an API via the `react-dom/test-utils` module (`https://facebook.github.io/react/docs/test-utils.html`), which we can use to assert that the component really renders everything we expect from it. With third-party package enzyme, we can do even more (`http://airbnb.io/enzyme/docs/api/shallow.html`). To get an idea about it, we add a test in the `Footer` suite--`./app/js/Components/Footer.spec.jsx`:

```
import { shallow } from "enzyme";
import * as manifest from "../../../package.json";

describe(

"Footer", () => {
  //...
  it( "renders manifest name", () => {
    const tree = shallow(

    <Footer />
    );
    expect ( tree.find( "footer" ).length ).toBe( 1 );
    expect( tree.find(

"footer" ).text().indexOf( manifest.name ) ).not.toBe( -1 );
  });
});
```

So, we assume that the component renders an HTML footer element (`tree.find( "footer" )`). We also check whether the footer contains the project name from the manifest:

```
PASS  app/js/Components/Footer.spec.jsx
  Footer
    ✓ matches previously saved snapshot (11ms)
    ✓ renders manifest name (9ms)

PASS  app/js/Components/Participants.spec.jsx
  Participants
    ✓ matches previously saved snapshot (8ms)

Test Suites: 2 passed, 2 total
Tests:       3 passed, 3 total
Snapshots:   2 passed, 2 total
Time:        2.317s
Ran all test suites.
```

Packaging and distribution

When we worked with File Explorer and NW.js, we used the `nwjs-builder` tool for packaging our application. The Electron has an even more sophisticated tool--electron-builder (`https://github.com/electron-userland/electron-builder`). Actually, it builds an application installer. The range of target package formats electron-builder supports is impressive. Then, why not try packaging our application? First, we install the tool:

```
npm i -D electron-builder
```

We add a new script to the manifest--`./package.json`:

```
"scripts": {
    ...
    "dist": "build"
},
```

We also set an arbitrary ID for the application in field build:

```
"build": {
    "appId": "com.example.chat"
},
```

We definitely want to provide the application with an icon, so we create the `build` subdirectory and place their `icon.icns` for macOS, `icon.ico` for Windows there. Icons for Linux will be extracted from `icon.icns`. Alternatively, you can place icons in `build/icons/` named after their sizes--`64x64.png`.

In fact, we have not yet granted our application window with an icon. To fix it, we modify our main process script--`./app/main.js`:

```
mainWindow = new BrowserWindow({
    width: 1000, height: 600, frame: false,
    icon: path.join(

__dirname, "icon-64x64.png
" )
});
```

Everything seems ready, so we can run the following:

```
npm run dist
```

As the process completes, we can find the generated package in the default format in the newly created `dist` folder:

- Ubuntu: `chat-1.0.0-x86_64.AppImage`
- * Windows: `chat Setup 1.0.0.exe`
- * MacOS: `chat-1.0.0.dmg`

Of course, we can aim for a specific target format:

```
build -l deb
build -w nsis-web
build -m pkg
```

Note that the diverse package format may require additional metadata in the manifest (`https://github.com/electron-userland/electron-builder/wiki/Options`). For instance, packaging in `.deb` requires both the `homepage` and `author` fields filled in.

Deployment and updates

Built-in capacities for auto updates is one of Electron's most prominent advantages over NW.js. Electron's `autoUpdater` module (`http://bit.ly/1KKdNQs`) utilizes the Squirrel framework (`https://github.com/Squirrel`), which makes *silent* possible. It works nicely in conjunction with the existing solution for multiplatform release servers; in particular, one can run it with Nuts (`https://github.com/GitbookIO/nuts`) using GitHub as a backend. We can also quickly set up a fully-featured node server based on `electron-release-server` (`https://github.com/ArekSredzki/electron-release-server`), which includes release management UI.

 Electron-updater doesn't support Linux. The project maintainers recommend using the distribution's package manager to update the application.

For the sake of brevity, we will walk through a simplified autoupdate approach that doesn't require a real release server, but only requires access to static releases via HTTP.

We start by installing the package:

```
npm i -S electron-updater
```

Now, we add to the manifest's `build` field--publish property:

```
"build": {
    "appId": "com.example.chat",
    "publish": [
        {
            "provider":

"generic",
            "url": "http://127.0.0.1:8080/"
        }
    ]
},
...
```

Here, we state that our `dist` folder will be available publicly on `127.0.0.1:8080`, and we go on with the `generic` provider. Alternatively, the provider can be set to Bintray (`https://bintray.com/`) or GitHub.

We modify our main process script to take advantage of the `electron-updater` API-- `./app/main.js`:

```
const { app, BrowserWindow, ipcMain } = require( "electron" ),
        { autoUpdater } = require( "electron-

updater" );

function send( event, text = "" ) {
  mainWindow && mainWindow.webContents.send(

event, text );
}

autoUpdater.on("checking-for-update", () => {
  send( "info", "Checking for

update..." );
});
autoUpdater.on("update-available", () => {
  send( "info", "Update not available" );


});
autoUpdater.on("update-not-available", () => {
  send( "info", "Update not available" );
});
```

```
autoUpdater.on("error", () => {
  send( "info", "Error in auto-updater" );
});
autoUpdater.on

("download-progress", () => {
  send( "info", "Download in progress..." );
});
autoUpdater.on

("update-downloaded", () => {
  send( "info", "Update downloaded" );
  send( "update-downloaded" );
});

ipcMain.on( "restart", () => {
  autoUpdater.quitAndInstall();
});
```

Basically, we subscribe for the `autoUpdater` events and report them to the renderer script using the `send` function. When `update-downloaded` is fired, we send the `update-downloaded` event to the renderer. The renderer on this event supposedly reports to the user about a newly downloaded version and asks whether it would be convenient to restart the application. When confirmed, the renderer sends the `restart` event. From the main process, we subscribe to it using `ipcMain` (http://bit.ly/2pChUNg). So, when `reset` is fired, `autoUpdater` restarts the application.

Note that `electron-debug` won't be available after packaging, so we have to remove it from the main process:

```
// require( "electron-debug" )();
```

Now, we make a few changes to the renderer script--`./app/index.html`:

```html
<!DOCTYPE html>
<html>
  <head>
    <meta charset="UTF-8">

<title>Chat</title>
    <link href="./assets/css/custom.css" rel="stylesheet" type="text/css"/>
  </head>
  <body>
    <app></app>
    <i id="statusbar"

class="statusbar"></i>
```

```
   </body>
   <script>
    require( "./build/renderer.js" );

// Listen for messages
const { ipcRenderer } = require( "electron" ),
      statusbar =

document.getElementById( "statusbar" );

ipcRenderer.on(  "info", ( ev, text ) => {

statusbar.innerHTML = text;
});
ipcRenderer.on(  "update-downloaded", () => {
  const ok = confirm

('The application will automatically restart to finish installing the
update');
  ok && ipcRenderer.send(

"restart" );
});

   </script>
</html>
```

In HTML, we add the `<i>` element with ID `statusbar`, which will print out reports from the main process. In JavaScript, we subscribe for main process events using `ipcRenderer` (`http://bit.ly/2p9xuwt`). On the `info` event, we change the content of the `statusbar` element with the event payload string. When `update-downloaded` occurs, we call `confirm` for the user opinion about a suggested restart. If the result is positive, we send the `restart` event to the main process.

Eventually, we edit CSS to stick our `statusbar` element in the left-bottom corner of the viewport--`./app/assets/css/custom.css`:

```
.statusbar {
  position: absolute;
  bottom: 1px;
  left: 6px;
}
```

Everything is done; let's rock it! So, we first rebuild the project and release it:

```
npm run build
npm run dist
```

We make the release available through HTTP using `http-server`
(https://www.npmjs.com/package/http- server):

```
http-server ./dist
```

We run the release to install the application. The application starts up as usual because no new releases are available yet, so we release a new version:

```
npm version patch
npm run build
npm run dist
```

 In the footer component, we display the application name and version taken by the `require` function from the manifest. Webpack retrieves it at compilation time. So, if `package.json` is modified after the application is built, the changes do not reflect in the footer; we need to rebuild the project.

 Alternatively, we can take the name and version dynamically from the app (http://bit.ly/2qDmdXj) object of Electron and forward it as an IPC event to the renderer.

Now, we will start our previously installed release and this time, we will observe the `autoUpdater` reports in `statusbar`. As the new release is downloaded, we will get the following confirmation window:

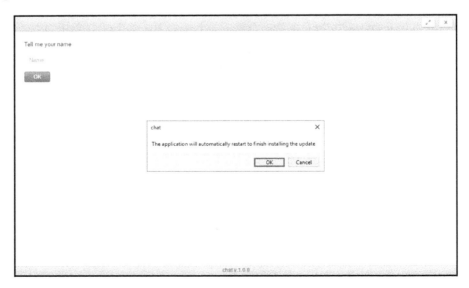

After pressing **OK**, the application closes and a new window showing the installation process pops up:

When it's done, start the updated application. Note that the footer now contains the latest released version:

Summary

We've completed our chat application. We started this chapter by programming the actions of the title bar. On the way, we learned how to control application window state in Electron. We looked into the WebSockets technology on the example of simple echo server and the accompanying client. Going deeper, we designed chat services based on WebSockets. We bound client events to the component states. We were introduced to the Jest testing framework and examined a generic approach to unit-testing React components. Besides, we created regression tests for both stateless and stateful components. We packaged our application and built an installer. We fiddled with publishing releases and made the application update whenever a new release is available.

5

Creating a Screen Capturer with NW.js, React, and Redux – Planning, Design, and Development

In this chapter, we are starting a new application—screen capturer. With this tool, will be able to take screenshots and record screencasts. We will build the application using the React components of the Material UI toolkit, which implements Google's Material Design specification. We already gained some experience with React while working on the chat example. Now, we are taking a step further towards scalable and highly maintainable application development. We are going to have an introduction to one of the hottest libraries of the time that called Redux, which manages the application state.

At the end of the chapter, we will have a prototype, which already responds to user actions, but misses the service to capture display input and save it in a file.

Application blueprint

This time, we will develop a screen capturer, a little tool capable of taking screenshots and recording screencasts.

The core idea can be expressed with the following user stories:

- As a user, I can take a screenshot and save it as a .png file
- As a user, I can start recording a screencast
- As a user, I can start recording the screencast and save it as .webm file

Additionally, I expect a notification to appear when a screenshot or screencast file is saved. I also would like to have the application presented in the system notification area (**Tray**) and to respond to specified global hot-keys. With a help of WireframeSketcher (http://wirefra mesketcher.com/), I illustrated my vision with the following wireframe:

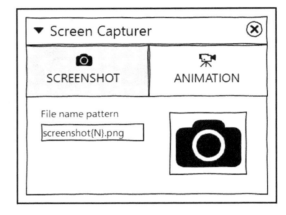

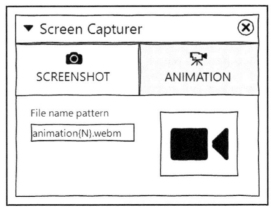

The wireframe implies a **Tabbed Document Interface** (TDI) with two panels. The first one, labeled as **Screenshot,** allows us to take a screenshot (photo icon) and set the filename pattern for the output file. The second panel (**Animation**) looks pretty much the same, except the action button is intended to start screencast recording. As soon as a user hits the button, it gets replaced with the stop recording button and vice versa.

Setting up the development environment

We will create this application with NW.js. As you may remember from Chapter 1, *Creating a File Explorer with NW.js - Planning, Designing, and Development* and Chapter 2, *Creating a File Explorer with NW.js – Enhancement and Delivery*, NW.js looks up the manifest file for the start page link and application window meta information:

`./package.json`

```
{
  "name": "screen-capturer",
  "version": "1.0.0",
  "description": "Screen Capturer",
  "main": "index.html",
  "chromium-args": "--mixed-context",
  "window": {
    "show": true,
    "frame": false,
    "width": 580,
    "height": 320,
    "min_width": 450,
    "min_height": 320,
    "position": "center",
    "resizable": true,
    "icon": "./assets/icon-48x48.png"
  }
}
```

This time, we do not need a big window. We go with `580x320px` and allow shrinking the window size down to `450x320px`. We set the window to open at the center of the screen without the frame and built-in windowing controls.

When we were setting up NW.js in the first two chapters, we had just a few dependencies. Now, we are going to take advantage of React and, therefore, we need the corresponding packages:

```
npm i -S react
npm i -S react-dom
```

As for dev dependencies, obviously, we need NW.js itself:

```
npm -i -D nw
```

Same as for the chat application that is also based on React, we will use Babel compiler and Webpack bundler. So, it gives us the following:

```
npm -i -D webpack
npm -i -D babel-cli
npm -i -D babel-core
npm -i -D babel-loader
```

As we remember Babel by itself is a platform, we need to specify what exact preset it applies to compile our sources. We already worked with these two:

```
npm -i -D babel-preset-es2017
npm -i -D babel-preset-react
```

Now, we extend the list with the `stage-3` preset (`https://babeljs.io/docs/plugins/preset-stage-3/`):

```
npm -i -D babel-preset-stage-3
```

This plugin set includes all the features of the so-called **Stage 3** proposal for the **EcmaScript** specification. In particular, it comprised of spread/rest operators on objects, which unlocks the most expressive syntax for the object composition.

In addition, we will apply two plugins not included in Stage 3:

```
npm -i -D babel-plugin-transform-class-properties
npm -i -D babel-plugin-transform-decorators-legacy
```

We are already familiar with the first one (ES Class Fields and Static Properties—`https://github.com/tc39/proposal-class-public-fields`). The second allows us to use decorators (`https://github.com/tc39/proposal-decorators`).

Since everything else is ready, we will extend the manifest file with automation scripts:

`package.json`

```
...
"scripts": {
    "start": "nw .",
    "build": "webpack",
    "dev": "webpack -d --watch"
  }
```

These targets have already been used while developing the chat application. The first one fires up the application. The second compiles and bundles sources. And the third one runs continuously and builds the project every time any of the source files change.

For bundling, we have to configure Webpack:

`./webpack.config.js`

```js
const { join } = require( "path" ),
      webpack = require( "webpack" );
      BUILD_DIR = join( __dirname, "build" ),
      APP_DIR = join( __dirname, "js" );


module.exports = {
  entry: join( APP_DIR, "app.jsx" ),
  target: "node-webkit",
  devtool: "source-map",
  output: {
      path: BUILD_DIR,
      filename:  "app.js"
  },
  module: {
    rules: [
      {
        test: /.jsx?$/,
        exclude: /node_modules/,
        use: [{
          loader: "babel-loader",
          options: {
            presets: [ "es2017", "react", "stage-3" ],
            plugins: [ "transform-class-properties", "transform-decorators-
legacy" ]
          }
        }]
      }
    ]
  }
};
```

So Webpack will start bundling ES6 modules recursively with `./js/app.jsx`. It will place the resulting JavaScript in `./build/app.js`. On the way, any `.js`/`.jsx` file requested for export will be compiled with Babel according to the configured presets and plugins.

Static prototype

The chat application we styled using CSS is provided by the Photon framework. This time, we are going to use ready-made React components of the Material-UI toolkit (`http://www.material-ui.com`). What we get as developers is reusable units confronting Google Material Design guidelines (`https://material.io/guidelines/`). It ensures a good look and feel as well as providing a unified experience on different platforms and device sizes. We can install Material-UI with `npm`:

```
npm i -S material-ui
```

According to Google Material Design requirements, the application shall support different devices, including mobile, where we need to handle specialized events, such as `on-tap`. Currently, React does not support them from the box; one has to use a plugin:

```
npm i -S react-tap-event-plugin
```

We do not intend to run our application on a mobile, but without the plugin, we are going to have warnings.

Now, when we are done with preparations, we can start scaffolding, as follows:

1. We add our startup HTML:

`./index.html`

```html
<!doctype html>
<html class="no-js" lang="">

<head>
  <meta charset="utf-8">
  <meta http-equiv="X-UA-Compatible" content="IE=edge">
  <title>Screen Capturer</title>
  <meta
    name="viewport"
    content="width=device-width, initial-scale=1, user-scalable=0, maximum-scale=1, minimum-scale=1"
  >
  <link
href="https://fonts.googleapis.com/icon?family=Material+Icons"
      rel="stylesheet">
  <link href="https://fonts.googleapis.com/css?family=Roboto"
rel="stylesheet">
  <link rel="stylesheet" type="text/css"
href="./assets/main.css">
</head>
```

```
<body>
  <root></root>
  <script src="./build/app.js"></script>
</body>

</html>
```

Here, in the `head` element, we link to three external stylesheets. The first one (`https://fonts.googleapis.com/icon?family=Material+Icons`) unlocks Material Icons (`https://material.io/icons/`). The second (`https://fonts.googleapis.com/css?family=Roboto`) brings the Roboto font that is extensively used in Material Design. The last one (`./assets/main.css`) is our customization CSS. In the body, we set the `root` container for the application. I decided, instead of a custom element for readability, we could use an ordinary `div` instead. At the end, we load the JavaScript (`./build/app.js`) generated by Webpack according to our configuration.

2. We add the custom styles that we have already referred in `main.css`:

`./assets/main.css`

```
html {
    font-family: 'Roboto', sans-serif;
}

body {
    font-size: 13px;
    line-height: 20px;
    margin: 0;
}
```

3. We create the entry point script:

`./js/app.jsx`

```
import React from "react";
import { render } from "react-dom";
import App from "./Containers/App.jsx";

render( <App />, document.querySelector( "root" ) );
```

Here, we import the `App` container component and render it into the `<root>` element of the DOM. The component itself will look as follows:

`./js/Containers/App.jsx`

```
import React, { Component } from "react";
import injectTapEventPlugin from "react-tap-event-plugin";
import Main from "../Components/Main.jsx";
import { deepOrange500 } from "material-ui/styles/colors";
import getMuiTheme from "material-ui/styles/getMuiTheme";
import MuiThemeProvider from "material-ui/styles/MuiThemeProvider";

injectTapEventPlugin();

const muiTheme = getMuiTheme({
  palette: {
    accent1Color: deepOrange500
  }
});

export default class App extends Component {
  render() {
    return (
        <MuiThemeProvider muiTheme={muiTheme}>
        <Main />
        </MuiThemeProvider>
    );
  }
}
```

At this point, we wrap the application pane (`Main`) with the Material UI theme provider. With the `getMuiTheme` function imported from the Material UI package, we describe the theme and pass the derived configuration to the provider. As mentioned previously, we have to apply `injectTapEventPlugin` to enable the custom events in React that are used by the framework.

Now is the time to add presentational components. We start with the main layout:

`./js/Components/Main.jsx`

```
import React, {Component} from "react";

import { Tabs, Tab } from "material-ui/Tabs";
import FontIcon from "material-ui/FontIcon";

import TitleBar from "./TitleBar.jsx";
import ScreenshotTab from "./ScreenshotTab.jsx";
```

```
import AnimationTab from "./AnimationTab.jsx";

class Main extends Component {

  render() {
    const ScreenshotIcon = <FontIcon className="material-
icons">camera_alt</FontIcon>;
    const AnimationIcon = <FontIcon className="material-
icons">video_call</FontIcon>;

    return (
      <div>
        <TitleBar />
        <Tabs>
          <Tab
            icon={ScreenshotIcon}
            label="SCREENSHOT"
          />
          <Tab
            icon={AnimationIcon}
            label="ANIMATION"
          />
        </Tabs>
        <div>

          { true
              ? <ScreenshotTab  />
              : <AnimationTab />
          }
        </div>

      </div>
    );
  }
}

export default Main;
```

This component comprises the title bar, two tabs (`Screenshot` and `Animation`), and conditionally, either the `ScreenshotTab` panel or `AnimationTab`. For rendering the tab menu, we apply the Material UI `Tabs` container and the `Tab` component for child items. We also use the `FontIcon` Material UI component to render Material Design icons. We assign icons declared at the beginning of the render method to corresponding tabs by using props:

`./js/Components/TitleBar.jsx`

```
import React, { Component } from "react";
```

```
import AppBar from 'material-ui/AppBar';
import IconButton from 'material-ui/IconButton';
const appWindow = nw.Window.get();

export default function TitleBar() {
  const iconElementLeft = <IconButton
      onClick={() => appWindow.hide()}
      tooltip="Hide window"
      iconClassName="material-icons">arrow_drop_down_circle</IconButton>,
        iconElementRight= <IconButton
      onClick={() => appWindow.close()}
      tooltip="Quit"
      iconClassName="material-icons">power_settings_new</IconButton>;

    return (<AppBar
      className="titlebar"
      iconElementLeft={iconElementLeft}
      iconElementRight={iconElementRight}>
      </AppBar>);

}
```

We implement the title bar with the `AppBar` Material UI component. Like in the previous example, we preliminarily define icons (this time, by using the `IconButton` component) and pass them to `AppBar` with props. We set inline handlers for the `IconButton` click event. The first one hides the window and the second closes the application. What is more, we set a custom CSS class `titlebar` to `AppBar`, because we are going to use this area as a window handle for drag and drop. So, we extend our custom style sheet:

`./assets/main.css`

```
...
.titlebar {
  -webkit-user-select: none;
  -webkit-app-region: drag;
}

.titlebar button {
  -webkit-app-region: no-drag;
}
```

Now, we need a component representing tab panels. We start with `ScreenshotTab`:

`./js/Components/ScreenshotTab.jsx`

```
import React, { Component } from "react";
```

```
import IconButton from "material-ui/IconButton";
import TextField from "material-ui/TextField";

const TAB_BUTTON_STYLE = {
  fontSize: 90
};

const SCREENSHOT_DEFAULT_FILENAME = "screenshot{N}.png";

export default class ScreenshotTab extends Component {

  render(){
    return (
      <div className="tab-layout">
        <div className="tab-layout__item">
          <TextField
              floatingLabelText="File name pattern"
              defaultValue={SCREENSHOT_DEFAULT_FILENAME}
          />

        </div>
        <div className="tab-layout__item">

          <IconButton
            tooltip="Take screenshot"
            iconClassName="material-icons"
            iconStyle={TAB_BUTTON_STYLE}>add_a_photo</IconButton>
        </div>
      </div>
    )
  }
}
```

Here, we use `IconButton` for the **Take a screenshot** action. We make it extra large by passing it with props custom styling (`TAB_BUTTON_STYLE`). In addition, we apply the `TextField` component to render text input in the style of Material Design.

The second tab panel will be quite similar:

./js/Components/AnimationTab.jsx

```
import React, { Component } from "react";
import IconButton from "material-ui/IconButton";
import TextField from "material-ui/TextField";

const TAB_BUTTON_STYLE = {
  fontSize: 90
};
```

```
const ANIMATION_DEFAULT_FILENAME = "animation{N}.webm";

export default class AnimationTab extends Component {

  render(){
    return (
      <div className="tab-layout">
          <div className="tab-layout__item">
            <TextField
                floatingLabelText="File name pattern"
                defaultValue={ANIMATION_DEFAULT_FILENAME}
              />
          </div>
          <div className="tab-layout__item">

{ true ? <IconButton
            tooltip="Stop recording"
            iconClassName="material-icons"
            iconStyle={TAB_BUTTON_STYLE}>videocam_off</IconButton>
            : <IconButton
            tooltip="Start recording"
            iconClassName="material-icons"
            iconStyle={TAB_BUTTON_STYLE}>videocam</IconButton> }
          </div>
        </div>
      )
  }
}
```

The only difference it makes here is the conditional rendering of either the `Start recording` button or `Stop recording`.

And that is pretty much everything for the static prototype. We just need to bundle the application:

```
npm run build
```

And fire it up:

```
npm start
```

You will get the following output:

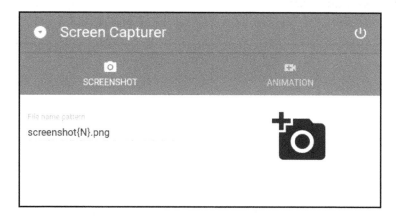

Comprehending redux

We learned to manage the component state while working on the chat application. It was quite sufficient for that small example. However, as the application grows larger, you may notice that multiple components tend to share the state. We know how to lift the state up. But which exact component then shall manage the state? Where does the state belong? We can avoid this ambiguity by drawing on Redux, a JavaScript library known as a predictable state container. Redux implies an application-wide state tree. When we need to set the state for a component, we update the corresponding node in the global state tree. All the subscribed modules immediately receive the updated state tree. Thus, we can always easily find out what is going on with the application by checking the state tree. We can save and restore the entire application state at will. Just imagine, with a little effort, we can implement time traveling through application state history.

I presume you are probably a bit confused now. The approach, if you have no experience with it or its predecessor Flux, may look strange. In fact, it's surprisingly easy to grasp when you start working with it. So, let's jump in.

Redux has three fundamental principles:

1. Everything that happens within the application is represented by a state.
2. The state is read-only.
3. State mutations are made with pure functions that take the previous state, dispatch action, and return the next state.

We receive new states by dispatching actions. An action is a plain object with the only mandatory field type that accepts a string. We are allowed to set as many arbitrary fields as we wish for the payload:

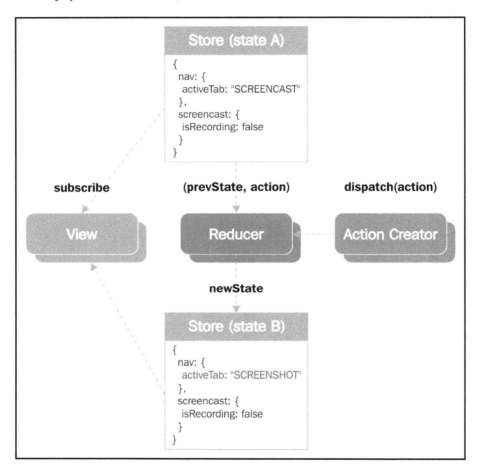

The preceding figure depicts the following flow:

1. We have the store in a particular state; let's say A.
2. We dispatch an action (created by a pure function, called **Action Creator**).
3. That invokes the **Reducer** function with arguments: state object (representing state A) and the dispatched action object.

4. The **Reducer** clones the supplied state object and modifies the clone object according to the scenario defined for the given action.

5. The **Reducer** returns the object representing the new store, **State B**.

6. Any component connected to the store receives the new state and calls the `render` method to reflect the state change in the view.

For example, in our application, we are going to have tabs. When a user clicks on all of them, the corresponding panel is supposed to show up. So, we need to represent the current `activeTab` in the state. We can do it as follows:

```
const action = {
  type: "SET_ACTIVE_TAB",
  activeTab: "SCREENSHOT"
};
```

However, we dispatch actions not directly, but via a function, which is called `actionCreator`:

```
const actionCreatorSetActiveTab = ( activeTab ) => {
  return {
    type: "SET_ACTIVE_TAB",
    activeTab
  };
};
```

The function takes zero or more input arguments and produces the action object.

The **Action** indicates that something happened, but doesn't change the state. That is a task of another function called **Reducer**. **Reducer** receives as a parameter of an object representing the previous state and the last dispatched action object. According to the action type and payload, it produces a new state object and returns it:

```
const initialState = {
  activeTab: ""
};

const reducer = ( state = initialState, action ) => {
  switch ( action.type ) {
    case "SET_ACTIVE_TAB":
      return { ...state, activeTab: action.activeTab };
    default:
      return state;
  }
};
```

In the previous example, we defined the initial application state in the constant `initialState`. We make it the default function parameter (https://mzl.la/2qgdNr6in) with the statement `state = initialState`. It means that when nothing is passed with the arguments, `state` takes the value of `initialState`.

Pay attention to how we get a new state object. We declare a new object literal. We are destructuring the previous state object in it and extending it with the `activeTab` key-value pair set from action payload. Reducer must be a pure function, so we could not change a value passed in the state object. You know that, with parameters, we receive `state` as a reference, so if we simply changed the value of the `activeTab` field in `state`, the corresponding object outside the function scope would have been impacted through the link. We have to ensure the previous state is immutable. So, we create a new object for that. Destructuring is a considerably new approach. If you do not feel comfortable with it, you can go with `Object.assign`:

```
return Object.assign( {}, state, { activeTab: action.activeTab } );
```

For our application, we will use the only reducer, but in general, we may have many. We can use the `combineReducers` function exported by `redux` to combine multiple reducers so that each of them represents a separate leave of the global state tree.

We pass to `createStore` function of `redux` the reducer (can be also a product of `combineReducers`). The function produces the store:

```
import { createStore } from "redux";
const store = createStore( reducer );
```

 If we render the React application on server-side, we can expose the state object into the JavaScript global scope (for example, `window.STATE_FROM_SERVER`) and connect it from the client: `const store = createStore( reducer, window.STATE_FROM_SERVER );`

And now is the most exciting part. We subscribe to store events:

```
store.subscribe(() => {
  console.log( store.getState() );
});
```

We will then dispatch an action:

```
store.dispatch( actionCreatorSetActiveTab( "SCREENSHOT" ) );
```

While dispatching, we created an action of the type SET_ACTIVE_TAB with activeTab set to SCREENSHOT in the payload. Therefore, console.log in the store update handler prints the new state updated accordingly:

```
{
  activeTab: "SCREENSHOT"
}
```

Introducing the application state

After this brief tour into Redux, we will apply the newly obtained knowledge in practice. First, we will install the redux package:

npm i –S redux

We will also use the additional helper library redux-act (https://github.com/pauldijou/redux-act) to simplify the declaration of action creators and reducers. By using this library, we can use the action creator functions as references within reducers, abandoning the switch(action.type) construction in favor of a shorter map syntax:

npm i –S redux-act

For screen capture, we should perform the following actions:

- SET_ACTIVE_TAB: It receives the identifier of the selected tab
- TOGGLE_RECORDING: It receives true when screencast recording starts and false when it ends
- SET_SCREENSHOT_FILENAME: It receives the output filename in the panel Screenshot
- SET_SCREENSHOT_INPUT_ERROR: It receives a message when an input error occurs
- SET_ANIMATION_FILENAME: It receives an output filename in the panel Animation
- SET_ANIMATION_INPUT_ERROR: It receives a message when an input error occurs

The implementation will look as follows:

`./js/Actions/index.js`

```
import { createStore } from "redux";
import { createAction } from "redux-act";

export const toggleRecording = createAction( "TOGGLE_RECORDING",
  ( toggle ) => ({ toggle }) );
export const setActiveTab = createAction( "SET_ACTIVE_TAB",
  ( activeTab ) => ({ activeTab }) );
export const setScreenshotFilename = createAction(
"SET_SCREENSHOT_FILENAME",
    ( filename ) => ({ filename }) );
export const setScreenshotInputError = createAction(
"SET_SCREENSHOT_INPUT_ERROR",
    ( msg ) => ({ msg }) );
export const setAnimationFilename = createAction( "SET_ANIMATION_FILENAME",
    ( filename ) => ({ filename }) );
export const setAnimationInputError = createAction(
"SET_ANIMATION_INPUT_ERROR",
  ( msg ) => ({ msg }) );
```

Instead of the canonical syntax, we have:

```
export const setActiveTab =  ( activeTab ) => {
  return {
    type: "SET_ACTIVE_TAB",
    activeTab
  };
}
```

We go here with a shorter one, achieved with the `createAction` function of `redux-act`:

```
export const setActiveTab = createAction( "SET_ACTIVE_TAB",
  ( activeTab ) => ({ activeTab }) );
```

Another function, `createReducer`, exported by `redux-act`, makes the reducer declaration even shorter:

`./js/Reducers/index.js`

```
import { createStore } from "redux";
import { createReducer } from "redux-act";
import * as Actions from "../Actions";
import { TAB_SCREENSHOT, SCREENSHOT_DEFAULT_FILENAME,
ANIMATION_DEFAULT_FILENAME } from "../Constants";
```

```
const DEFAULT_STATE = {
  isRecording: false,
  activeTab: TAB_SCREENSHOT,
  screenshotFilename: SCREENSHOT_DEFAULT_FILENAME,
  animationFilename: ANIMATION_DEFAULT_FILENAME,
  screenshotInputError: "",
  animationInputError: ""
};

export const appReducer = createReducer({
  [ Actions.toggleRecording ]: ( state, action ) => ({ ...state,
isRecording: action.toggle }),
  [ Actions.setActiveTab ]: ( state, action ) => ({ ...state, activeTab:
action.activeTab }),
  [ Actions.setScreenshotFilename ]: ( state, action ) => ({ ...state,
screenshotFilename: action.filename }),
  [ Actions.setScreenshotInputError ]: ( state, action ) => ({ ...state,
screenshotInputError: action.msg }),
  [ Actions.setAnimationFilename ]: ( state, action ) => ({ ...state,
animationFilename: action.filename }),
  [ Actions.setAnimationInputError ]: ( state, action ) => ({ ...state,
animationInputError: action.msg })
}, DEFAULT_STATE );
```

We do not need to describe reducer conditioning with a switch statement like we did during Redux's introduction:

```
const reducer = ( state = initialState, action ) => {
  switch ( action.type ) {
    case "SET_ACTIVE_TAB":
      return { ...state, activeTab: action.activeTab };
    default:
      return state;
  }
};
```

The function createReducer does it for us:

```
export const appReducer = createReducer({
  [ Actions.setActiveTab ]: ( state, action ) => ({ ...state, activeTab:
action.activeTab }),
}, DEFAULT_STATE );
```

The function takes in a map-like object, where we use action creator functions as keys (for example, [Actions.setActiveTab]). Yeah, for dynamic object keys, we have to go with the syntax called **Computed property names** at https://mzl.la/2erqyrj. As object values, we use callbacks to generate the new state.

In this sample, we clone the old state (`{...state}`) and change in the derived object `activeTab` property value.

If you noted, we used imports from `Constants/index.js`. In that module, we are going to encapsulate the application scope constants:

`./js/Constants/index.js`

```
export const TAB_SCREENSHOT = "TAB_SCREENSHOT";
export const TAB_ANIMATION = "TAB_ANIMATION";
export const SCREENSHOT_DEFAULT_FILENAME = "screenshot{N}.png";
export const ANIMATION_DEFAULT_FILENAME = "animation{N}.webm";
```

Well, we have actions and a reducer. That's the time to create the store and connect it to the application:

`./js/Containers/App.jsx`

```
import React from "react";
import { render } from "react-dom";
import { createStore } from 'redux';
import { Provider } from "react-redux";
import App from "./Containers/App.jsx";
import { appReducer } from "./Reducers";

const store = createStore( appReducer );

render(<Provider store={store}>
  <App />
 </Provider>, document.querySelector( "root" ) );
```

We build the store using the `createStore` function of `redux`. Then, we wrap the `App` component with `Provider` provided by the `react-redux` package. Do not forget to install the dependency:

npm i -S react-redux

The **Provider** takes in a previously created store with props and makes it available for another `react-redux` function, `connect`. We will use this function in our `App` container component:

`./js/Containers/App.jsx`

```
//...
import { connect } from "react-redux";
import { bindActionCreators } from "redux";
import * as Actions from "../Actions";
```

```
const mapStateToProps = ( state ) => ({ states: state });
const mapDispatchToProps = ( dispatch ) => ({
  actions: bindActionCreators( Actions, dispatch )
});

class App extends Component {
  render() {
    return (
        <MuiThemeProvider muiTheme={muiTheme}>
        <Main {...this.props} />
        </MuiThemeProvider>    );
  }
}

export default connect( mapStateToProps, mapDispatchToProps)( App );
```

Here, we define two mapper functions that `connect` accepts as arguments. The first `mapStateToProps` maps the stored state to the props. With the statement `( state ) => ({ states: state })`, we make the store state available in the component as `this.props.states`. The second `mapDispatchToProps` maps our actions to the props. The callback receives automatically from the `connect` function `dispatch` bound to the store. Together with the function `bindActionCreators` of `redux`, we can use it to map a set of actions to the props. So, we imported all the available actions as a plain object, `Actions`, and passed it to `bindActionCreators`. The return is mapped to the `actions` field, and therefore will be available within the component as `this.props.actions`.

Finally, we pass the component to a function produced by `connect`. It extends the component, which we export upstream. This expression may look a bit confusing. Actually, what we do here is we modify the behavior of the component without explicitly modifying the component itself. Traditionally, in OOP languages, we used to achieve it with the Decorator pattern (`https://en.wikipedia.org/wiki/Decorator_pattern`). Nowadays, many languages have built-in capacities, such as attributes in C#, annotations in Java, and decorators in Python. ECMAScript also has a proposal, `https://tc39.github.io/proposal-decorators/`, for decorators. Thus, by using the declarative syntax, we can modify the shape of a class or a method without touching its code. The plugin `babel-plugin-transform-decorators-legacy`, which we used in our Webpack configuration unlocks this feature to us. So, we can already use it for connecting the component to the store:

```
@connect( mapStateToProps, mapDispatchToProps )
export default class App extends Component {
  render() {
    return (
        <MuiThemeProvider muiTheme={muiTheme}>
```

```
        <Main {...this.props} />
      </MuiThemeProvider>      );
  }
}
```

From the container, we render the `Main` component and pass to it all the props of the container (by destructuring the parent props `{...this.props}`). So, `Main` receives the mapped state and actions in the props. We can use the following:

`./js/Components/Main.jsx`

```
import React, {Component} from "react";
import { Tabs, Tab } from "material-ui/Tabs";
import FontIcon from "material-ui/FontIcon";

import TitleBar from "./TitleBar.jsx";
import ScreenshotTab from "./ScreenshotTab.jsx";
import AnimationTab from "./AnimationTab.jsx";
import { TAB_SCREENSHOT, TAB_ANIMATION } from "../Constants";


class Main extends Component {
  onTabNav = ( tab ) => {
    const { actions } = this.props;
    return () => {
      actions.setActiveTab( tab );
    };
  }

  render() {
    const ScreenshotIcon = <FontIcon className="material-
icons">camera_alt</FontIcon>;
    const AnimationIcon = <FontIcon className="material-
icons">video_call</FontIcon>;
    const { states, actions } = this.props;

    return (
      <div>
        <TitleBar />
        <Tabs>
          <Tab
            onClick={this.onTabNav( TAB_SCREENSHOT )}
            icon={ScreenshotIcon}
            label="SCREENSHOT"
          />
          <Tab
            onClick={this.onTabNav( TAB_ANIMATION )}
            icon={AnimationIcon}
```

```
        label="ANIMATION"
      />
    </Tabs>
    <div>

      { states.activeTab === TAB_SCREENSHOT
          ? <ScreenshotTab {...this.props} />
          : <AnimationTab {...this.props} />
      }
    </div>

  </div>
 );
 }
}

export default Main;
```

As you remember, this component serves the tab menu. We subscribe here for the *click on tab* events. We do not subscribe to the handler directly, but a function, `this.onTabNav`, bound to the instance scope that produces the intended handler according to the passed-in tab key. The constructed handler receives the key with the closure and passes it to the `setActiveTab` action creator extracted from `this.props.actions`. The action gets dispatched and the global state changes. From the component's perspective, it is like calling `setState`, which causes the component to update. The `activeTab` field extracted from `this.props.state` changes its value respectively and the component renders the panel matching the key passed with `this.onTabNav`.

As for the panel, we can already connect the filename form to the state:

`./js/Components/ScreenshotTab.jsx`

```
import React, { Component } from "react";
import IconButton from "material-ui/IconButton";
import TextField from "material-ui/TextField";
import { TAB_BUTTON_STYLE, SCREENSHOT_DEFAULT_FILENAME } from
"../Constants";

export default class ScreenshotTab extends Component {
  onFilenameChange = ( e ) => {
    const { value } = e.target;
    const { actions } = this.props;
    if ( !value.endsWith( ".png" ) || value.length < 6 ) {
      actions.setScreenshotInputError( "File name cannot be empty and must
end with .png" );
      return;
    }
```

```
            actions.setScreenshotInputError( "" );
            actions.setScreenshotFilename( value );
    }

    render(){
        const { states } = this.props;
        return (
            <div className="tab-layout">
                <div className="tab-layout__item">
                    <TextField
                        onChange={this.onFilenameChange}
                        floatingLabelText="File name pattern"
                        defaultValue={SCREENSHOT_DEFAULT_FILENAME}
                        errorText={states.screenshotInputError}
                    />

                </div>
                <div className="tab-layout__item">

                    <IconButton
                        tooltip="Take screenshot"
                        iconClassName="material-icons"
                        iconStyle={TAB_BUTTON_STYLE}>add_a_photo</IconButton>
                </div>
            </div>
        )
    }
}
```

Here, we subscribe the `this.onFilenameChange` handler for the `change` event on `TextField`. So, if the user types in `this.onFilenameChange` it invokes and validates the input. If the current value is less than six characters in length or does not end with `.png`, it is considered as invalid. So, we use the `setScreenshotInputError` action creator extracted from `this.props.actions` to set a value for the error message. As soon as it is done, the `screenshotInputError` field of the state changes as well as the `errorText` property of the `TextField` component, and the error message shows up. If the filename is valid, we dispatch the `setScreenshotInputError` action to reset the error message. We change the screenshot filename in the state tree by calling the action creator `setScreenshotFilename`.

If you have noticed, we encapsulated the `IconButton` custom style in the constants module, so it could be shared between both panels. But we have to add the new constant to the module:

`./js/Constants/index.js`

```
export const TAB_BUTTON_STYLE = {
  fontSize: 90
};
```

The second panel, in addition to form validation, also changes the state field `isRecording`:

`./js/Components/AnimationTab.jsx`

```
import React, { Component } from "react";
import IconButton from "material-ui/IconButton";
import TextField from "material-ui/TextField";
import { TAB_BUTTON_STYLE, ANIMATION_DEFAULT_FILENAME } from
"../Constants";

export default class AnimationTab extends Component {
  onRecord = () => {
    const { states } = this.props;
    this.props.actions.toggleRecording( true );
  }
  onStop = () => {
    this.props.actions.toggleRecording( false );
  }
  onFilenameChange = ( e ) => {
    const { value } = e.target;
    const { actions } = this.props;
    if ( !value.endsWith( ".webm" ) || value.length < 7 ) {
      actions.setAnimationInputError( "File name cannot be empty and must
end with .png" );
      return;
    }
    actions.setAnimationInputError( "" );
    actions.setAnimationFilename( value );
  }

  render(){
    const { states } = this.props;
    return (
      <div className="tab-layout">
          <div className="tab-layout__item">
              <TextField
                  onChange={this.onFilenameChange}
                  floatingLabelText="File name pattern"
```

```
                        defaultValue={ANIMATION_DEFAULT_FILENAME}
                        errorText={states.animationInputError}
                    />
                </div>
                <div className="tab-layout__item">


        { states.isRecording ? <IconButton
                    onClick={this.onStop}
                    tooltip="Stop recording"
                    iconClassName="material-icons"
                    iconStyle={TAB_BUTTON_STYLE}>videocam_off</IconButton>
                    : <IconButton
                    onClick={this.onRecord}
                    tooltip="Start recording"
                    iconClassName="material-icons"
                    iconStyle={TAB_BUTTON_STYLE}>videocam</IconButton> }
                </div>
            </div>
        )
    }
}
```

We subscribe the handlers for click events on both the **Start recording** and **Stop recording** buttons. When a user hits the first one, the this.onRecord handler invokes the action creator, toggleRecording, which sets the state field isRecording to true. It causes the component to update. According to the new state, it replaces the **Start recording** button with the **Stop recording** one. And vice versa, if **Stop recording** is clicked in the this.onStop handler, we call toggleRecording to set the state property isRecording to false. The component updates respectively.

Now, we can build the application and run it:

```
npm run build
npm start
```

Observe that when we are switching tabs, editing file names, or toggling start/stop recording, the application responds as we intend.

Summary

In this chapter, we familiarized ourselves with the basics of Google's Material Design. We built the static prototype from ready-made React components of the Material-UI set. We had an introduction into the Redux state container. We defined our application state tree and set state mutators. We created the global state store and connected it to the container component. We passed exposed action creators and state tree trunk into presentation components with the props. We examined shorter action/reducer declaration syntaxes provided by the `redux-act` library. We implemented it by using Redux state machine actions, such as tabbed navigation, recording toggle, and form validation.

6

Creating a Screen Capturer with NW.js: Enhancement, Tooling, and Testing

In Chapter 5, *Creating a Screen Capturer with NW.js, React, and Redux – Planning, Design, and Development*, we applied the Redux store to manage the application state. Now, we are going to get a look at how to use middleware for tooling Redux and how to unit-test Redux.

The main goal of this chapter though is to eventually teach our Screen Capturer to take screenshots and record screencasts. For that, you will learn how to use WebRTC APIs to capture and record a media stream. We will examine generating a still frame image from the stream by using canvas. We will put in practice the Notification API to inform the user about actions performed regardless of what window is in focus. We will add a menu to the system tray and bind it with the application state. We will make capturing action available via global keyboard shortcuts.

Tooling Redux

In Chapter 5, *Creating a Screen Capturer with NW.js, React and Redux Planning, Design and Development*, you have learned the essentials of the Redux state container. We built a functional prototype using Redux. However, when building your own application, you may need to know when and what is happening to the state tree exactly.

Fortunately, Redux accepts middleware modules to deal with cross-cutting concerns. The concept is pretty similar to the one of the Express framework. We can extend Redux by hooking third-party modules on the event when an action gets dispatched but hasn't yet reached the reducers. It doesn't make much sense to write a custom logger as many are already available (`http://bit.ly/2qINXML`). For example, for tracing changes in the state tree, we can use the `redux-diff-logger` module that reports only the state diffs, which makes it much easier to read. So, we will install the package (`npm i -S redux-diff-logger`) and add a few lines to the entry script:

`./js/app.jsx`

```
import { createStore, applyMiddleware, compose } from "redux";
import logger from 'redux-diff-logger';
const storeEnhancer = compose(
      applyMiddleware( logger )
    );
const store = createStore( appReducer, storeEnhancer );
```

Here, we export `logger` from `redux-diff-logger` and pass it in the `applyMiddleware` function of the `redux` module to create a store enhancer. The store enhancer applies a given middleware to the `dispatch` method of the store. With the `compose` function of `redux`, we can combine multiple enhancers. We pass the derivative as the second argument to the `createStore` function.

Now, we can build the project and start it up. We play a bit with the UI and take a look in **DevTools**. The JavaScript console panel will output the state diffs we caused:

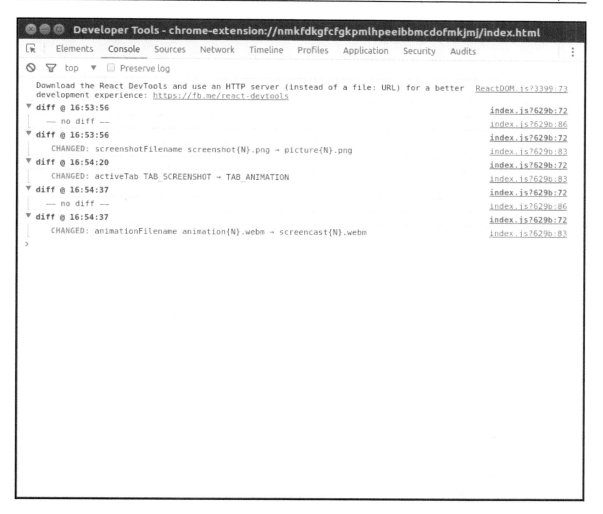

Though the redux-diff-logger middleware we receive reports in the JavaScript console of DevTools as we perform any action causing state change. For example, we modified screenshot filename template and that immediately reflected in the console. In fact we received a whole new object for the state tree, but redux-diff-logger is smart enough to show us only what really interested in - the diff of the state.

Redux DevTools

Logging reports is already something, but it would be more useful if we could get a tool like `DevTools` to interact with the state. Third-party package `redux-devtools` brings in an extensible environment, which supports state live-editing and time traveling. We will examine it in conjunction with two additional modules, `redux-devtools-log-monitor` and `redux-devtools-dock-monitor`. The first allows us to inspect the state and time travel. The second is a wrapper that docks the Redux DevTools UI to window edges when we press the corresponding hot-key. To see it in action, we create a new component out of custom describing DevTools:

`./js/Components/DevTools.jsx`

```
import React from "react";
import { createDevTools } from "redux-devtools";
import LogMonitor from "redux-devtools-log-monitor";
import DockMonitor from "redux-devtools-dock-monitor";


const DevTools = createDevTools(
  <DockMonitor toggleVisibilityKey="ctrl-h"
               changePositionKey="ctrl-q"
               defaultPosition="bottom"
               defaultIsVisible={true}>
    <LogMonitor theme="tomorrow" />
  </DockMonitor>
);
export default DevTools;
```

We use the `createDevTools` function to create the component. It takes in JSX, where we configure visibility and the position of React DevTools UI through the props of `DockMonitor` and color theme in `LogMonitor`.

The derived component exposes the method instrument, which returns as a store enhancer. So, we can pass it to the compose function:

`./js/app.jsx`

```
import DevTools from "./Components/DevTools.jsx";
const storeEnhancer = compose(
      applyMiddleware( logger ),
      DevTools.instrument()
    );
const store = createStore( appReducer, storeEnhancer );
```

In the `DevTools` component itself, we have to add it to the DOM:

```
render(<Provider store={store}>
  <div>
    <App />
    <DevTools />
  </div>
</Provider>, document.querySelector( "root" ) );
```

Now, when we run the application, we can see the dock. We can press *Ctrl + Q* to change its position and *Ctrl + H* to hide or to show it:

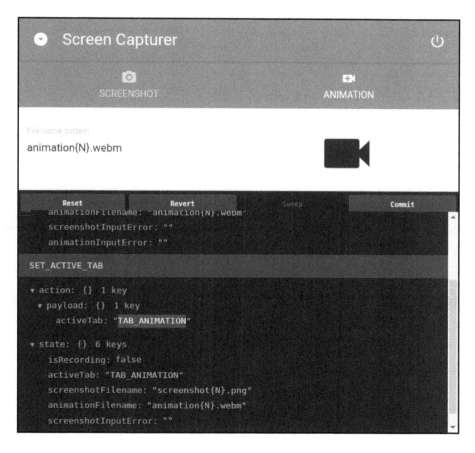

Unit-testing Redux

We have already fiddled with the Jest testing framework in `Chapter 4`, *Chat System with Electron and React: Enhancement, Testing, and Delivery (Writing Unit-tests section)*. Redux introduces new concepts, such as actions and reducers. Now, we are going to unit-test them.

As you may remember, to run Jest, we need to configure Babel:

`.babelrc`

```
{
  "presets": [
    ["env", {
      "targets": { "node": 7 },
      "useBuiltIns": true
    }],
    "react",
    "stage-3"
  ],
  "plugins": [
    "transform-class-properties",
    "transform-decorators-legacy"
  ]
}
```

Again, with `env` preset, we target Babel on Node.js 7 and enable the extra plugins we used in the webpack configuration.

Testing action creator

Actually, that's quite simple with action creators because they are pure functions. We pass in an input according to the function interface and verify the output:

`./js/Actions/index.spec.js`

```
import { createStore } from "redux";
import { toggleRecording } from "./index";
describe( "Action creators", () => {
  describe( "toggleRecording", () => {
    it( "should return a valid action", () => {
      const FLAG = true,
            action = toggleRecording( FLAG );
            expect( action.payload ).toEqual( { toggle: FLAG } );
    });
```

```
    });
  });
```

We have written a test for the `toggleRecording` function. We assert the fact that the function produces an action object with `{ toggle: FLAG }` in the payload. As mentioned in the previous chapter, any action is supposed to have a mandatory property `type`. When we omit the description while calling the `createAction` function of the `redux-act` module, the derived action creator will produce an action with dynamically generated identifiers, which is hardly testable. However, we give it a string as the first argument, for example, `TOGGLE_RECORDING`:

```
const toggleRecording = createAction( "TOGGLE_RECORDING", ( toggle ) =>
({ toggle }) );
this becomes the unique identifier and therefore we can expect it in type
property.
expect( action.type ).toEqual( "TOGGLE_RECORDING" );
```

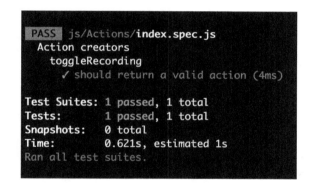

Pretty much the same way we can test every action creator in our current application.

Testing reducers

Reducers, as well as action creators, are pure functions. They accept the last state tree object and the dispatched action in parameters and produce a new state tree object. So, when testing a reducer, we are checking whether a given action modifies the state as intended:

`./js/Reducers/index.spec.js`

```
import { createStore } from "redux";
import { createReducer } from "redux-act";
import { TAB_SCREENSHOT, SCREENSHOT_DEFAULT_FILENAME,
ANIMATION_DEFAULT_FILENAME } from "../Constants";
import { appReducer } from "./index";
```

```
describe( "appReducer", () => {
  it( "should return default state", () => {
    const DEFAULT_STATE = {
      isRecording: false,
      activeTab: TAB_SCREENSHOT,
      screenshotFilename: SCREENSHOT_DEFAULT_FILENAME,
      animationFilename: ANIMATION_DEFAULT_FILENAME,
      screenshotInputError: "",
      animationInputError: ""
    };
    expect( appReducer() ).toEqual( DEFAULT_STATE );
  });
});
```

For the very first time, Redux calls our reducer with the undefined state. What we expect from the reducer is to take a predefined object as the default state. So, if we call the function with no arguments, it is supposed to receive at entry point the default state and return it without modifications as no action was given.

On the other hand, we can import an action creator:

```
import { toggleRecording } from "../Actions";
```

Create an action and pass it to the reducer:

```
it( "should return a new state for toggleRecording action", () => {
  const FLAG = true,
        action = toggleRecording( FLAG ),
        newState = appReducer( undefined, action );
  expect( newState.isRecording ).toEqual( FLAG );
});
```

Thus, we test that the reducer produces a new state, changed in accordance with the given action. An action is created by calling toggleRecording(true) is supposed to set the state object property isRecording to true. That is what we assert in the test:

```
PASS  js/Actions/index.spec.js
  Action creators
    toggleRecording
      ✓ should return a valid action (4ms)

PASS  js/Reducers/index.spec.js
  appReducer
    ✓ should return default state (1ms)
    ✓ should return a new state for toggleRecording action (1ms)

Test Suites: 2 passed, 2 total
Tests:       3 passed, 3 total
Snapshots:   0 total
Time:        0.649s, estimated 1s
Ran all test suites.
```

Taking a screenshot

The previously created static prototype may look fancy, but is not of much use. We need a service capable of taking screenshots and recording screencasts.

If it was about a screenshot of the application window, we would simply use the API on NW.js:

```
import * as fs from "fs";
function takeScreenshot( filePath ){
  appWindow.capturePage(( img ) => {
    fs.writeFileSync( filePath, img, "base64" );
  }, {
    format : "png",
    datatype : "raw"
  });
}
```

But we need a screenshot of the screen and, therefore, we have to get access to display input. W3C includes a specification draft, "Media Capture and Streams" (http://bit.ly/2qTtLXX), which describes an API to capture displayed media (mediaDevices.getDisplayMedia). Unfortunately, at the time of writing, it's not yet supported in NW.js or, to be honest, by any browser. However, we can still use webkitGetUserMedia, which streams the desktop input. This API was once a part of technology known as WebRTC (https://webrtc.org), designed for real-time video, audio, and data communication.

Yet, currently, it is removed from the specification, but still available in both NW.js and Electron. It seems like we don't really have a choice, so we go with it.

`webkitGetUserMedia` takes in the so-called `MediaStreamConstraints` object describing what we want to capture and returns a promise. In our case, the constraints object may look as follows:

```
{
    audio: false,
    video: {
     mandatory: {
       chromeMediaSource: "desktop",
       chromeMediaSourceId: desktopStreamId,
       minWidth: 1280,
       maxWidth: 1920,
       minHeight: 720,
       maxHeight: 1080
     }
    }
}
```

We disable audio recording, set boundaries for video (`webkitGetUserMedia` determines a suitable size based on your display resolution. When the resolution does not fit the range it causes `OverconstrainedError`), and describe the media source. But we need a valid media stream ID. That we can obtain, for example, from the NW.js API:

```
nw.Screen.chooseDesktopMedia([ "window", "screen" ], ( mediaStremId ) => {
    // mediaStremId
});
```

When combining all together, we get the following service:

`./js/Service/Capturer.js`

```
import * as fs from "fs";
const appWindow = nw.Window.get();
export default class Capturer {
  constructor(){
    nw.Screen.chooseDesktopMedia([ "window", "screen" ], ( id) => {
      this.start( id );
    });
  }
  takeScreenshot( filename ){
    console.log( "Saving screensho" );
  }
  start( desktopStreamId ){
    navigator.webkitGetUserMedia({
```

```
      audio: false,
      video: {
        mandatory: {
          chromeMediaSource: "desktop",
          chromeMediaSourceId: desktopStreamId,
          minWidth: 1280,
          maxWidth: 1920,
          minHeight: 720,
          maxHeight: 1080
        }
      }
    }, ( stream ) => {
      // stream to HTMLVideoElement
    }, ( error ) => {
      console.log( "navigator.getUserMedia error: ", error );
    });
  }
}
```

When running it, we get a dialog prompting us to choose a media source:

I do not really like this UX. I would rather make it detect desktop media. We achieve that with the following method:

```
static detectDesktopStreamId( done ){
    const dcm = nw.Screen.DesktopCaptureMonitor;
    nw.Screen.Init();
    // New screen target detected
    dcm.on("added", ( id, name, order, type ) => {
      // We are interested only in screens
      if ( type !== "screen" ){
        return;
      }
      done( dcm.registerStream( id ) );
      dcm.stop();
    });
    dcm.start( true, true );
}
```

We use `DesktopCaptureMonitor` of the NW.js API for detecting available media devices, rejecting an app window (the type `"screen"`), and obtaining the media stream ID with the method `registerStream`. Now, we replace the `chooseDesktopMedia` of the NW.js API with our custom method, `detectDesktopStreamId`:

```
constructor(){
  Capturer.detectDesktopStreamId(( id ) => {
    this.start( id );
  });
}
```

Well we manage to receive the stream. We have to direct it somewhere. We can create a hidden `HTMLVideoElement` and use it as a video stream receiver. We encapsulate this functionality in a separate module:

`./js/Service/Capturer/Dom.js`

```
export default class Dom {
  constructor(){
    this.canvas = document.createElement("canvas")
    this.video = Dom.createVideo();
  }
   static createVideo(){
    const div = document.createElement( "div" ),
          video = document.createElement( "video" );
    div.className = "preview";
    video.autoplay = true;
    div.appendChild( video );
    document.body.appendChild( div );
```

```
      return video;
  }
}
```

During construction, the class creates a new DIV container and video element in it. The container gets attached to the DOM. We also need to support the new elements with CSS:

`./assets/main.css`

```css
.preview {
  position: absolute;
  left: -999px;
  top: -999px;
  width: 1px;
  height: 1px;
  overflow: hidden;
}
```

Basically, we move the container out of view. So, the video will be streamed into a hidden `HTMLVideoElement`. The task is now to capture a still frame and convert it into an image. That we can do with the following trick:

```js
getVideoFrameAsBase64() {
  const context = this.canvas.getContext("2d"),
        width = this.video.offsetWidth,
        height = this.video.offsetHeight;
  this.canvas.width = width;
  this.canvas.height = height;
  context.drawImage( this.video, 0, 0, width, height );
  return this.canvas.toDataURL("image/png")
    .replace( /^data:image\/png;base64,/, "" );
}
```

We create a canvas context matching the video size. By using the context method `drawImage`, we draw an image from the video stream. Finally, we convert canvas to Data URI and obtain the Base64-encoded image by striping the `data:scheme` prefix.

We are going to inject our `Dom` module instance in the `Capturer` service as a dependency. For that, we need to modify the constructor:

`./js/Service/Capturer.js`

```js
constructor( dom ){
    this.dom = dom;
    Capturer.detectDesktopStreamId(( id ) => {
      this.start( id );
    });
```

```
    }
```

We also have to forward the media stream into `HTMLVideoElement`:

```
start( desktopStreamId ){
    navigator.webkitGetUserMedia( /* constaints */, ( stream ) => {
        this.dom.video.srcObject = stream;
    }, ( error ) => {
        console.log( "navigator.getUserMedia error: ", error );
    });
}
```

We also add a method for saving screenshots:

```
takeScreenshot( filename ){
    const base64Data = this.dom.getVideoFrameAsBase64();
    fs.writeFileSync( filename, base64Data, "base64" );
}
```

Now, when this method is called in a component, the image gets saved silently. To tell the truth, it's not very user-friendly. A user presses the button and receives no information about whether the image really is saved or not. We can improve user experience by showing a desktop notification:

```
const ICON = `./assets/icon-48x48.png`;
//...
takeScreenshot( filename ){
    const base64Data = this.dom.getVideoFrameAsBase64();
    fs.writeFileSync( filename, base64Data, "base64" );
    new Notification( "Screenshot saved", {
        body: `The screenshot was saved as ${filename}`,
        icon: `./assets/icon-48x48.png`
    });
}
```

Now, when the newly created screenshot is saved, the corresponding message gets displayed at the system level. So, even if the application window is hidden (for example, we use system tray or a shortcut), the user still receives a notification:

Recording a screencast

In fact, while building the service for taking screenshots, we have done most of the work for screencast recording. We already have the `MediaStream` object delivered by `webkitGetUserMedia`. We just need a way to define the start and end of recording and save the collected frames in a video file. That is where we can benefit from the `MediaStream` Recording API, which captures the data produced by `MedaStream` or `HTMLMediaElement` (for example, `<video>`) so that we can save it. So, we modify the service again:

`./js/Service/Capturer.js`

```
//...
const toBuffer = require( "blob-to-buffer" );
//...
start( desktopStreamId ){
    navigator.webkitGetUserMedia(/* constaints */, ( stream ) => {
        let chunks = [];
        this.dom.video.srcObject = stream;
        this.mediaRecorder = new MediaRecorder( stream );
        this.mediaRecorder.onstop = ( e ) => {
            const blob = new Blob( chunks, { type: "video/webm" });
            toBuffer( blob, ( err, buffer ) => {
                if ( err ) {
                    throw err;
                }
                this.saveAnimationBuffer( buffer );
                chunks = [];
            });
        }
        this.mediaRecorder.ondataavailable = function( e ) {
            chunks.push( e.data );
        }
    }, ( error ) => {
        console.log( "navigator.getUserMedia error: ", error );
    });
}
```

After receiving `MediaStream`, we use it to make an instance of `MediaRecorder`. We subscribe for the `dataavailable` event on the instance. The handler accepts a Blob (a file-like object representing a frame of the stream). To make a video, we need a sequence of the frames. So, we push every received Blob into the chunks array. We also subscribe a handler for the stop event, which creates a new Blob of the type `webm` from the collected chunks. Thus, we have a Blob representing the screencast, but we can't just save it in a file.

For a stream of binary data, Node.js will expect from us an instance of the Buffer class. We use the `blob-to-buffer` package to convert Blob to Buffer.

In this code, we rely on two events, `dataavailable` and `stop`. The first one gets fired when we start the recorder and the second when we stop it. These actions we make public:

```
record( filename ){
    this.mediaRecorder.start();
    this.saveAnimationBuffer = ( buffer ) => {
      fs.writeFileSync( filename, buffer, "base64" );
      new Notification( "Animation saved",  {
        body: `The animation was saved as ${filename}`,
        icon: ICON
      });
    }
  }
  stop(){
    this.mediaRecorder.stop();
  }
```

When the method `record` is called, the instance of `MediaRecorder` starts recording and, on the contrary, with the `stop` method, it ceases the process. In addition, we define `saveAnimationBuffer` callback that will be called when recording stops (`this.mediaRecorder.onstop`). The callback (`saveAnimationBuffer`) receives with the `buffer` parameter the binary stream of the recorded screencast and saves it with the `writeFileSync` method of the `fs` core module. Similar to a screenshot, on saving a screencast, we create a desktop notification to inform the user about the performed action.

The service is almost ready. But as you can remember from our wireframes, the Screen Capturer accepts a template for the filename, such as `screenshot{N}.png` or `animation{N}.webm`, where `{N}` is a placeholder for the file index. Therefore, I would like to encapsulate filesystem operations in the dedicated class, `Fsys`, where we can process the template as needed:

`./js/Service/Capturer/Fsys.js`

```
import * as fs from "fs";
export default class Fsys {
  static getStoredFiles( ext ){
    return fs.readdirSync( "." )
      .filter( (file) => fs.statSync( file ).isFile()
        && file.endsWith( ext ) ) || [ ];
  }
  saveFile( filenameRaw, data, ext ){
    const files = Fsys.getStoredFiles( ext ),
        // Generate filename of the pattern like screenshot5.png
```

```
        filename = filenameRaw.replace( "{N}", files.length + 1 );
      fs.writeFileSync( filename, data, "base64" );
      return filename;
    }
  }
```

This class has the static method `getStoredFiles`, which returns an array of all the files of a given type (extension) from the working directory. Before saving a file in the `saveFile` method, we get the list of the earlier stored files and calculate the value for `{N}` as `files.length + 1`. Thus, the very first screenshot will be saved under the name `screenshot1.png`, the second as `screenshot2.png`, and so on.

The `Fsys` instance we inject in the `Capturer` service:

```
export default class Capturer {
  constructor( fsys, dom ){
    this.fsys = fsys;
    this.dom = dom;
    Capturer.detectDesktopStreamId(( id ) => {
      this.start ( id );
    });
  }
```

We will instantiate the service in the entry script:

`./func-services/js/app.jsx`

```
  import Fsys from "./Service/Capturer/Fsys";
  import Dom from "./Service/Capturer/Dom";
  import Capturer from "./Service/Capturer";
  const capturer = new Capturer( new Fsys(), new Dom() );
  render(<Provider store={store}>
    <App capturer={capturer} />
  </Provider>, document.querySelector( "root" ) );
```

We import the `Capturer` class and the dependencies. While constructing `Capturer`, we pass it in the instances of `Fsys` and `Dom`. The derived instance of `Capturer` we pass with the props to the `App` component.

So, the instance of the service arrives into the `ScreenshotTab` component and we can use it for taking a screenshot:

`./js/Components/ScreenshotTab.jsx`

```
  // Handle when clicked CAPTURE
  onCapture = () => {
    const { states } = this.props;
```

```
            this.props.capturer.takeScreenshot( states.screenshotFilename );
        }
```

Similarly, in `AnimationTab`, we apply the methods record and stop of the instance from the corresponding handlers:

`./js/Components/AnimationTab.jsx`

```
    // Handle when clicked RECORD
    onRecord = () => {
        const { states } = this.props;
        this.props.capturer.record( states.animationFilename );
        this.props.actions.toggleRecording( true );
    }
    // Handle when clicked STOP
     onStop = () => {
        this.props.capturer.stop();
        this.props.actions.toggleRecording( false );
    }
```

Now, after building the application, we can use it to take a screenshot and record screencasts:

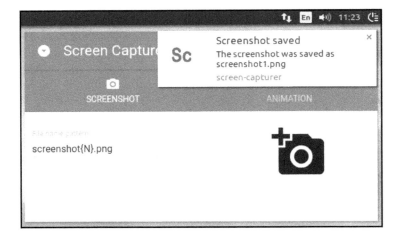

From our image, we can observe that the buttons to take screenshots and record screencasts are parts of the window UI. However, we also need to provide functionality for hiding a window. So how do we reach capturing actions while application is hidden? The answer is to do with system tray.

Taking advantage of the system tray

In Chapter 2, *Creating a File Explorer with NW.js – Enhancement and Delivery* , we already examined adding and managing the application menu in the system tray. Briefly, we created menu items with nw.MenuItem, added them to the nw.Menu instance, and attached the menu to nw.Tray. So, the boilerplate for the tray menu may look as follows:

./js/Service/Tray.js

```
const appWindow = nw.Window.get();
export default class Tray {
  tray = null;
  constructor( ) {
    this.title = nw.App.manifest.description;
    this.removeOnExit();
  }
  getItems = () => {
    return [ /* */ ];
  }
  render(){
    if ( this.tray ) {
      this.tray.remove();
    }
    const icon = "./assets/" +
      ( process.platform === "linux" ? "icon-48x48.png" : "icon-
      32x32.png" );
    this.tray = new nw.Tray({
      title: this.title,
      icon,
      iconsAreTemplates: false
    });
    const menu = new nw.Menu();
    this.getItems().forEach(( item ) => menu.append( new nw.MenuItem(
    item )));
    this.tray.menu = menu;
  }
  removeOnExit(){
    appWindow.on( "close", () => {
      this.tray.remove();
      appWindow.hide(); // Pretend to be closed already
      appWindow.close( true );
    });
    // do not spawn Tray instances on page reload
    window.addEventListener( "beforeunload", () => this.tray.remove(),
    false );
  }
}
```

For this application, we need the following menu items:

```
Take screenshot
Start recording
Stop recording
---
Open
Exit
```

Here, `Start recording` and `Stop recording` get enabled depending on the state `isRecording` property. Besides, we need the `Capturer` instance and state properties `screenshotFilename` and `animationFilename` to run the capturing action on user request. So, we inject both dependencies in the `Tray` constructor:

`./js/Service/Tray.js`

```
import { toggleRecording } from "../Actions";
import { SCREENSHOT_DEFAULT_FILENAME, ANIMATION_DEFAULT_FILENAME } from
"../Constants";
export default class Tray {
 // default file names
  screenshotFilename = SCREENSHOT_DEFAULT_FILENAME;
  animationFilename = ANIMATION_DEFAULT_FILENAME;
  isRecording = false;
  constructor( capturer, store ) {
    this.capturer = capturer;
    this.store = store;
}
```

In addition, we defined a few instance properties. `screenshotFilename` and `animationFilename` will receive the latest user-defined filename templates from the state. The property `isRecording` will take in the corresponding value of the state when it changes. In order to receive state updates, we subscribe for store changes:

```
constructor( capturer, store ) {
    //...
    store.subscribe(() => {
      const { isRecording, screenshotFilename, animationFilename } =
      store.getState();
      this.screenshotFilename = screenshotFilename;
      this.animationFilename = animationFilename;
      if ( this.isRecording === isRecording ) {
        return;
      }
      this.isRecording = isRecording;
      this.render();
    });
```

```
}
```

In the callback, we compare the actual `isRecording` value from the state with the earlier store one in the instance property `isRecording`. This way, we know when `isRecording` has really changed. Only then, we update the menu.

Finally, we can populate the array of menu items options in the `getItems` method:

```
getItems = () => {
    return [
        {
            label: `Take screenshot`,
            click: () => this.capturer.takeScreenshot(
            this.screenshotFilename )
        },
        {
            label: `Start recording`,
            enabled: !this.isRecording,
            click: () => {
                this.capturer.record( this.animationFilename );
                this.store.dispatch( toggleRecording( true ) );
            }
        },
        {
            label: `Stop recording`,
            enabled: this.isRecording,
            click: () => {
                this.capturer.stop();
                this.store.dispatch( toggleRecording( false ) );
            }
        },
        {
            type: "separator"
        },
        {
            label: "Open",
            click: () => appWindow.show()
        },
        {
            label: "Exit",
            click: () => appWindow.close()
        }
    ];
}
```

We use the `close` method of the application window to quit and the method `show` to restore the window if it is hidden. We rely on passed in the `Capturer` instance for capturing actions. We also update the state by dispatching (`store.dispatch`) the `toggleRecording` action.

Now we instantiate the `Tray` class in entry script and call it the `render` method:

`./js/app.jsx`

```
import Shortcut from "./Service/Shortcut"
const tray = new Tray( capturer, store );
tray.render();
```

When running the application, we can see in the system notification area the Screen Capturer menu:

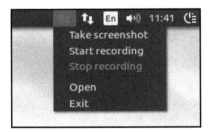

Registering global keyboard shortcuts

Menu in tray is a solution, but actually, we have an option to perform capturing actions even without opening the menu. NW.js allows us to assign global keyboard shortcuts:

```
const shortcut = new nw.Shortcut({
    key: "Shift+Alt+4",
    active: () => {}
    failed: console.error
  });
nw.App.registerGlobalHotKey( shortcut );
appWindow.on( "close", () => nw.App.unregisterGlobalHotKey( shortcut ) );
window.addEventListener( "beforeunload", () =>
nw.App.unregisterGlobalHotKey( shortcut ), false );
```

We use `nw.Shortcut` to create an object representing a shortcut. With `nw.App.registerGlobalHotKey`, the shortcut is registered. We use `nw.App.unregisterGlobalHotKey` to unregister the shortcut when the application closes or reloads.

That brings us to the following service:

`./js/Service/Shortcut.js`

```
const appWindow = nw.Window.get();
import { toggleRecording } from "../Actions";
import { SCREENSHOT_DEFAULT_FILENAME, ANIMATION_DEFAULT_FILENAME,
  TAKE_SCREENSHOT_SHORTCUT, RECORD_SHORTCUT, STOP_SHORTCUT } from
"../Constants";
export default class Shortcut {
 screenshotFilename = SCREENSHOT_DEFAULT_FILENAME;
 animationFilename = ANIMATION_DEFAULT_FILENAME;
 isRecording = false;

 constructor( capturer, store ) {
    this.capturer = capturer;
    this.store = store;
    store.subscribe(() => {
      const { isRecording, screenshotFilename, animationFilename } =
      store.getState();
      this.screenshotFilename = screenshotFilename;
      this.animationFilename = animationFilename;
      this.isRecording = isRecording;
    });
 }
 registerOne( key, active ){
    const shortcut = new nw.Shortcut({
      key,
      active,
      failed: console.error
    });
    // Register global desktop shortcut, which can work without focus.
    nw.App.registerGlobalHotKey( shortcut );
    appWindow.on( "close", () => nw.App.unregisterGlobalHotKey(
    shortcut ) );
    window.addEventListener( "beforeunload", () =>
    nw.App.unregisterGlobalHotKey( shortcut ), false );
 }
 registerAll(){
  this.registerOne( TAKE_SCREENSHOT_SHORTCUT, () =>
  this.capturer.takeScreenshot( this.screenshotFilename ) );
  this.registerOne( RECORD_SHORTCUT, () => {
```

```
      if ( this.isRecording ) {
        return;
      }
      this.capturer.record( this.animationFilename );
      this.store.dispatch( toggleRecording( true ) );
    });
    this.registerOne( STOP_SHORTCUT, () => {
      if ( !this.isRecording ) {
        return;
      }
      this.capturer.stop();
      this.store.dispatch( toggleRecording( false ) );
    });
  }
}
```

Pretty much like in the `Tray` class, we inject capturer and store instances. With the first one, we access capturing actions, and use the second to access the global state. We subscribe for state changes to get actual values for filename templates and `isRecording`. The method `registerOne` creates and registers a shortcut instance based on the given key and callback, and subscribes for the `close` and `beforeunload` events to unregister the shortcut. In the method `registerAll`, we declare our action shortcuts. The shortcuts key we will define in the constants module:

`./js/Constants/index.js`

```
export const TAKE_SCREENSHOT_SHORTCUT = "Shift+Alt+4";
export const RECORD_SHORTCUT = "Shift+Alt+5";
export const STOP_SHORTCUT = "Shift+Alt+6";
```

Now, we can also append the keys to tray menu items:

```
getItems = () => {
  return [
    {
      label: `Take screenshot (${TAKE_SCREENSHOT_SHORTCUT})`,
    //...
```

Now, when we run the application, we get the following tray menu:

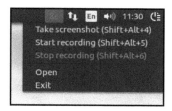

We can hide the application by hitting the Hide window (left hand-side) button of the title bar and take screenshots by pressing *Shift + Alt + 4* and screencasts, with *Shift + Alt + 5* and *Shift + Alt + 6* for starting and stopping recording, respectively.

Summary

We started this chapter by introducing the Redux middleware. As an example, we used `redux-diff-logger` to monitor mutations in the store. We also plugged in a collection of tools (`redux-devtools`), enabling DevTools-like panels on a page for inspecting the store and traveling back in time using the cancelling actions. Closing with Redux, we examined unit-testing of action creators and reducers.

In this chapter, we created the `Capturer` service responsible for taking screenshots and recording screencasts. We achieved capturing of desktop video input in `MediaStream` by using `webkitGetUserMedia` API. With the Canvas API, we managed to take a still frame from the video stream and convert it into an image. For video recording, we went with the `MediaRecorder` API. Both screenshot and screencast actions we have provided with the corresponding desktop notifications. We implemented an application menu in the system tray and bound it to the store. To access capturing actions even without opening the tray menu, we registered global keyboard shortcuts.

7

Creating RSS Aggregator with Electron, TypeScript , React, and Redux: Planning, Design, and Development

Wading through the previous chapters, we created an application with pure JavaScript, React and React + Redux. We are now coming to the optimal technology stack for large scalable web applications--TypeScript + React + Redux. We are going to develop the RSS Aggregator. I find it a good example to show TypeScript in action as well as to examine asynchronous actions. Besides, you will learn to use a new component library, React MDL. We will also extend it with custom styles written in SASS language.

Application blueprint

We develop a typical tool that aggregates syndicated content from a manageable list of sources. If we split the requirements into user stories, we will get something like this:

- As a user, I can see the list of earlier added sources
- As a user, I can see the aggregated content
- As a user, I can filter the content items by selecting a source in the menu

Let's again use **WireframeSketcher** (`http://wireframesketcher.com/`) and put it on a wireframe:

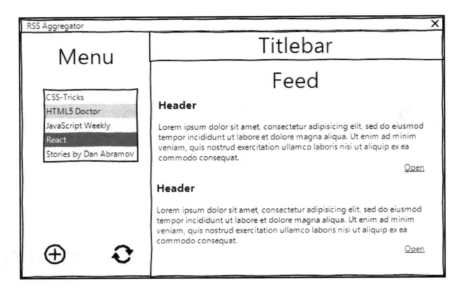

- As a user, I can open the item link next to the list

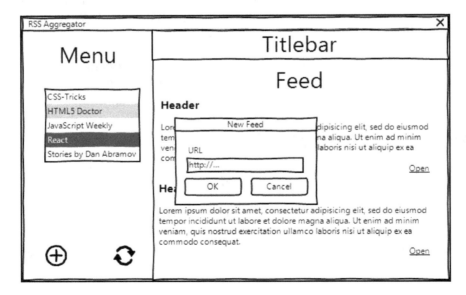

- As a user, I can add a source
- As a user, I can remove a source
- As a user, I can update aggregated content

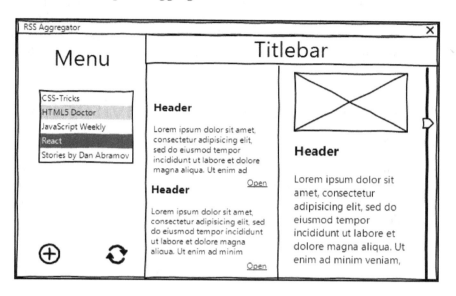

Welcome to TypeScript

When working on a large scalable application, it's essential that established architecture has been followed by all the team members. In other languages, such as Java, C++, C#, and PHP, we can declare types and interfaces. So, no one can go with a new functionality unless it fully satisfies the interface intended by the system architect. JavaScript has neither strict types nor interfaces. That why, in 2012, engineers of Microsoft developed a superset of JavaScript (ES2015) called **TypeScript.** This language extends JavaScript with optional static typing and compiles back to JavaScript, so is acceptable by any browser and operating system. It is similar to how we compile ES.Next to ECMAScript of the fifth edition with Babel, but in addition, brings us features that are unlikely to be integrated into ECMAScript in the foreseeable future. The language is exceptionally great and is documented at `https://www.typescriptlang.org/docs/home.html` and provided with an excellent specification `http://bit.ly/2qDmdXj`. The language is supported by the mainstream IDEs and code editors, and can be integrated through plugins in automation tools, such as Grunt, Gulp, Apache Maven, Gradle, and others. Some major frameworks are considering migrating to TypeScript, while Angular 2+ and Dojo 2 have already embraced it. Other frameworks expose their interfaces to TypeScript through definition files.

Alternatively for static type checking, one can go with **Flow** (`https://flow.org`) by Facebook. Unlike TypeScript, Flow is no compiler, but a checker. Basic typings in Flow are pretty similar to the ones of TypeScript, achieved by almost the same syntax. Flow also introduces advanced types, such as array, union, intersection, and generics, but does it in its own ways. According to Facebook, they created Flow because "TypeScript isn't built around bug finding as much as they wanted."

Setting up the development environment for TypeScript

TypeScript makes alluring promises regarding one's development experience. Why not fiddle with the code to see it in practice? First, we have to create a dedicated directory for upcoming samples. We initialize the project by running `npm init -y` and install `typescript` as a dev dependency:

```
npm i -D typescript
```

In the manifest `scripts` section, we add a command to compile sources with TypeScript:

`package.json`

```
{
...
"scripts": {
    "build": "tsc"
  },
...
}
```

We need to let TypeScript know what exactly we want from it. We will describe that in the configuration file:

`tsconfig.json`

```
{
  "compilerOptions": {
    "target": "ES6",
    "module": "CommonJS",
    "moduleResolution": "node",
    "sourceMap": true,
    "outDir": "./build"
  },
```

```
    "include": [
      "./**/*"
    ],
    "exclude": [
      "node_modules"
    ]
}
```

Here, we set the TypeScript compiler to search for `ts` sources anywhere within the project directory except `node_modules`. In `compilerOptions`, we specify how we want it to treat our sources during compilation. Field `target` is set in `ES6`, meaning TypeScript will compile into the ES6/ES2016 syntax, which is already fully supported in all the modern browsers. In the field `module`, we have `CommonJS`. Thus, TypeScript will bundle sources into CommonJS-compliant modules that play nicely with the Node.js environment. With the field `moduleResolution`, we choose in favor of the Node.js modules resolution style. In the field `outDir`, we determine where TypeScript will store the compiled modules. More information about compiler options is available at `http://bit.ly/2t9fckV`.

Basic types

The development environment now seems ready, so we can try it out with an elementary example:

example.ts

```
    let title: string = "RSS Aggregator";
```

We use the type annotation feature of TypeScript to set a constraint on the variable. That's so easy; we just extend the declaration with the so-called **declaration space** like `:type`, where type can be one of the basic types (boolean, number, string, array, void, any, and a few others), class, interface, type alias, enum, and import. Here, we applied `string`, meaning title accepts only strings.

After compiling with `npm run build`, we can find file `example.js` in the `./build` directory with the following content:

build/example.js

```
    let title = "RSS Aggregator";
```

You see it doesn't do much; it simply removes the type hinting. That's something amazing about TypeScript - type checking happens at compilation time and disappears by runtime. So, we benefit from TypeScript without any impact on the application's performance.

Well, let's do a nasty thing and set a value to the variable violating the given constraint:

example.ts

```
let title: string = "RSS Aggregator";
title = 1;
```

On compilation, we receive an error message:

```
error TS2322: Type '1' is not assignable to type 'string'.
```

Hmm; TypeScript warns us when we do something wrong. What is even more exciting is if your IDE supports TypeScript, you get notified on the fly while typing. I suggest to check against the list http://bit.ly/2a8rmTl and pick up the most suitable IDE for you if, by chance, yours isn't there. I would recommend **Alm** (http://alm.tools) as a great example of using TypeScript, React, and Redux together. However, I, myself, pulled in **NetBeans** (https://netbeans.org/) a decade ago and it has never disappointed me. It does not have native TypeScript support, but one can easily get it by installing the **TypeScript Editor plugin** (https://github.com/Everlaw/nbts).

Let's play with type annotation more. We take a function and define a contract for entry and exit points:

example.ts

```
function sum( a: number, b: number ): number {
  return a + b;
}
 let res = sum( 1, 1 );
console.log( res );
```

Actually, we state here that the function accepts two numbers and shall return a number. Now, if we even think of giving the function any type different from number, the IDE immediately alerts us about it:

Array, plain objects, and indexable types

Well, I believe, with primitive types, it's more or less clear, but what about the others, for example, arrays? By combining basic type with `[]`, we define an array type:

```
let arr: string[];
```

Here, we declare the variable `arr` that is an array of string. We can achieve the same with the following syntax:

```
let arr: Array<string>;
```

Alternatively, we can do it with interface:

```
interface StringArray {
  [ index: number ]: string;
}
 const arr: StringArray = [ "one", "two", "tree" ];
```

While declaring the `StringArray` interface by using the so-called **index signature**, we set constraints on the type structure. It accepts numeric indexes and string values. In other words, it's a string array. We can go further and set a constraint on the array length:

```
interface StringArray {
  [ index: number ]: string;
  length: number;
}
```

As for plain objects, we can go with an interface describing the intended shape:

```
interface MyObj {
  foo: string;
  bar: number;
}
let obj: MyObj;
```

On the other hand, we can set constraints inline with the object type literal:

```
let obj: { foo: string, bar: number };
// or
function request( options: { uri: string, method: string } ): void {
}
```

If we are able to declare a value object (http://bit.ly/2khKSBg), we need to ensure immutability. Fortunately, TypeScript allows us to specify that members of an object are readonly:

```
interface RGB {
    readonly red: number;
    readonly green: number;
    readonly blue: number;
}
 let green: RGB = { red: 0, green: 128, blue: 0 };
```

We can access a percentage, for example, red in a color of the RGB type. But we cannot change the RGB levels for a declared color. If we try this, we will get an error as follows:

```
error TS2540: Cannot assign to 'red' because it is a constant or a read-
only property.
```

For an object of arbitrary properties, we can use an index signature to target string keys:

```
interface DataMap {
  [ key: string ]: any;
}

const map: DataMap = { foo: "foo", bar: "bar" };
```

Note that, in DataMap, we set any for member type. By this, we allow any value types.

Function type

We can set constraints on a function by using the function type literal:

```
const showModal: (toggle: boolean) => void =
  function( toggle )   {
    console.log( toggle );
  }
```

I find it quite discouraging and prefer to use interface:

```
interface Switcher {
  (toggle: boolean): void;
}

const showModal:Switcher = ( toggle ) => {
  console.log( toggle );
}
```

```
showModal( true );
```

You may now ask, what if the function has optional parameters? TypeScript makes it very simple to define an optional parameter. You just need to append the parameter with a question mark:

```
function addOgTags(title: string, description?: string): string {
  return `
    <meta property="og:title" content="${title}" />
    <meta property="og:description" content="${description || ""}" />
  }
```

We made `description` optional, so we can call the function both ways:

```
addOgTags( "Title" );
addOgTags( "Title", "Description" );
```

None of these violates the declared interface; so far, we give it string.

In pretty much the same way, we can define optional object members:

```
interface IMeta {
  title: string;
  description?: string;
}

function addOgTags( meta: IMeta ): string {
}
```

Class type

In other languages, we are used to considering interfaces as closely related to classes. TypeScript brings a similar development experience. What is more, while Java and PHP interfaces cannot contain instance properties, TypeScript has no such limitations:

```
interface Starship {
  speed: number;
  speedUp( increment: number ): void;
}

class LightFreighter implements Starship {
  speed: number = 0;
  speedUp( increment: number ): void {
    this.speed = this.speed + increment;
  }
}
```

```
let millenniumFalcon = new LightFreighter();
millenniumFalcon.speedUp( 100 );
```

With the advance of ES2015/2016, classes are used widely in JavaScript. Yet, TypeScript allows us to set member accessibility. So, we declare a member as public when we permit access to it from the code consuming object instance. We use private to ensure the member will not be accessible outside its containing class. In addition, the protected members are similar to private, except they can be accessed in any of the derived class instances:

```
class LightFreighter implements Starship {
  private speed: number = 0;
  public speedUp( increment: number ): void {
    this.speed = this.speed + increment;
  }
}
```

As you can see, the value for speed is hardcoded. It would be just proper if our class could be configured for the initial speed during initialization. Let's do the refactoring:

```
class LightFreighter implements Starship {
  constructor( private speed: number = 0 ) {
  }
  public speedUp( increment: number ): void {
    this.speed = this.speed + increment;
  }
}
```

Here, we use another nice feature of TypeScript that I am personally excited about. It's called **parameter property**. We often declare private properties and populate them from constructor parameters. In TypeScript, we can simply prepend the parameter with an accessibility modifier and it will result in a respectively named property taking in the value of the parameter. So, in the previous code, using private speed in the parameter list, we declare the speed parameter and assign a passed in value to it. By using the ES6 syntax for the default parameter, we set speed to zero when nothing has passed in the constructor constructor(speed = 0).

Abstract classes

Similar to what you might be used to in other languages, in TypeScript, we can use abstract classes and methods. The abstract class is meant only for extending. One cannot create instances of the abstract class. Methods defined as abstract are required for implementation in any subclasses:

```
abstract class Starship {
  constructor( protected speed: number = 0 ) {

  }
  abstract speedUp( increment: number ): void;
}

class LightFreighter extends Starship {

  public speedUp( increment: number ): void {
    this.speed = this.speed + increment;
  }
}
```

Abstract classes are quite similar to interfaces, except a class can implement multiple interfaces, but extend only one abstract class.

Enum type

Time after time, we use constants to define a set of logically related entities. With TypeScript, we can declare an enumerated type populated with immutable data and then refer to the whole set by the type:

```
const enum Status {
    NEEDS_PATCH,
    UP_TO_DATE,
    NOT_INSTALLED
}

function setStatus( status: Status ) {
  // ...
}

setStatus( Status.NEEDS_PATCH );
```

Here, we declare a type `Status` that accepts one of the predefined values (`NEEDS_PATCH`, `UP_TO_DATE`, and `NOT_INSTALLED`). The function `setStatus` expects the `status` parameter to be of the `Status` type. If you pass in any other value, TypeScript reports an error:

```
setStatus( "READY" );
// error TS2345: Argument of type '"READY"' is not assignable to parameter
of type 'STATUS'.
```

Alternatively, we can use a string literal type that refers to any string value of a group:

```
function setStatus( status: "NEEDS_PATCH" | "UP_TO_DATE" | "NOT_INSTALLED"
) {
  // ...
}
setStatus( "NEEDS_PATCH" );
```

Union and intersection types

Interesting so far, isn't it? What would you say then to it: in TypeScript, we can refer to multiple types at once. For example, we have two interfaces `Anakin` and `Padmé` and need a new type (`Luke`) that inherits from both of them. We can achieve it as easily as this:

```
interface Anakin {
  useLightSaber: () => void;
  useForce: () => void;
}
interface Padmé {
  leaderSkills: string[];
  useGun: () => void;
}
type Luke = Anakin & Padmé;
```

Besides, we can do the intersection without explicitly declaring the type:

```
function joinRebelion( luke: Anakin & Padmé ){
}
```

We can also define a union type that allows any type of a group. You know the jQuery library, right? The function jQuery accepts for a selector parameter a number of diverse types and returns the jQuery instance. How could it possibly be covered with an interface?

```
interface PlainObj {
  [ key: string ]: string;
}
interface JQuery {
}

function jQuery( selector: string | Node | Node[] | PlainObj | JQuery ):
JQuery {
  let output: JQuery = {}
  // ...
  return output;
}
```

When a function returns a type depending on a passed-in type, we can declare an interface that describes all the possible use cases:

```
interface CreateButton {
  ( tagName: "button" ): HTMLButtonElement;
  ( tagName: "a" ): HTMLAnchorElement;
}
```

A function implementing this interface accepts a string for the tagName parameter. If the value is "button", the function returns the Button element. If "a", then it returns the Anchor element.

 One can find available DOM-related interfaces in the specification at
https://www.w3.org/TR/DOM-Level-2-HTML/html.html.

Generic type

The types we have just examined refer to a concrete type combination. In addition, TypeScript supports a so-called **generic type** that helps reusing the once created interface in different contexts. For example, if we want an interface for a data map, we can make it like this:

```
interface NumberDataMap {
  [ key: string ]: number;
}
```

But this `NumberDataMap` accepts only numbers for the member values. Let's say, for string values, we have to create a new interface, such as `StringDataMap`. Alternatively, we can declare a generic `DataMap` that sets an arbitrary value type constraint when referred:

```
interface DataMap<T> {
  [ key: string ]: T;
}

const numberMap: DataMap<number> = { foo: 1, bar: 2 },
      stringMap: DataMap<string> = { foo: "foo", bar: "bar" };
```

Global libraries

Yeah, TypeScript is, indeed, an impressive language when it comes to writing a new code. But what about existing none-TypeScript libraries? For example, we are going to use React and Redux modules. They are written in JavaScript, not in TypeScript. Luckily, mainstream libraries are already provided with TypeScript declaration files. We can install these files per module using npm:

```
npm i -D @types/react
npm i -D @types/react-dom
```

Now, when we try something stupid with any of these modules, we get immediately notified about the problem:

```
import * as React from "react";
import * as ReactDOM from "react-dom";

ReactDOM.render(
  <div></div>,
  "root"
);
```

On compiling or even while typing, you will get the error:

```
error TS2345: Argument of type '"root"' is not assignable to parameter of
type 'Element'.
```

Fair enough; instead of the HTML element (for example, `document.getElementById( "root" )`) I passed to `ReactDOM.render` a string as the second parameter.

Yet, to be honest, not every library is provided with TypeScript declarations. For example, in the *RSS Aggregator* application, I am going to use the `feedme` library (`https://www.npmjs.com/package/feedme`) to fetch and parse RSS by a URL. As it happens, the library has no declaration file. Fortunately, we can quickly create one:

`feedme.d.ts`

```
declare class FeedMe {
  new ( flag?: boolean ): NodeJS.WritableStream;
  on( event: "title", onTitle: ( title: string ) => void): void;
  on( event: "item", onItem: ( item: any ) => void ): void;
}
```

The module `feedme` exposes a class `FeedMe`, but TypeScript doesn't know about these modules; it is not yet declared in the TypeScript scope. So, we use ambient declaration in `feedme.d.ts` (`declare class FeedMe`) to introduce a new value in the scope. We state the class constructor that accepts an optional flag of the type `boolean` and returns the Node.js `WriteStream` object. We use overloading to describe two cases of function usage. In the first, it receives a string `"title"` for `event` and expects a callback for handling the RSS title. In the second, it takes in the event `"title"` and then expects a callback to handle the RSS entry.

Now, we can consume the newly created declaration file from the service:

```
/// <reference path="./feedme" />
import http = require( "http" );
var FeedMe = require( "feedme" );

http.get('http://feeds.feedburner.com/TechCrunch/startups', ( res ) => {
  const parser = new FeedMe( true );
  parser.on( "title", ( title: string ) => {
    console.log( title );
  });
  res.pipe( parser );
});
```

Using a triple-slash directive, we include `feedme.d.ts` in the project. After it's done, TypeScript validates if `FeedMe` is used according to its interface.

Creating static prototype

I assume, at this point, we are quite enough into TypeScript to start with the application. As with to the previous examples, first what we do is the static prototype.

Setting up the development environment for the application

We have to set up our development environment for the project. So, we dedicate a directory and put the following manifest there:

`./package.json`

```
{
  "name": "rss-aggregator",
  "title": "RSS Aggregator",
  "version": "1.0.0",
  "main": "./app/main.js",
  "scripts": {
    "build": "webpack",
    "start": "electron .",
    "dev": "webpack -d --watch"
  }
}
```

As requested by any Electron application, we set the path to our main process script in the `main` field. We also define scripts commands to run Webpack for building and for watching. We set one scripts command for running the application with Electron. Now, we can install the dependencies. We definitely need TypeScript, as we are going to build the application using it:

```
npm i -D typescript
```

For bundling, we will use Webpack as we did for Chat and for Screen Capturer applications, but this time, instead of `babel-loader`, we go with `ts-loader`, because our sources are in the TypeScript syntax:

```
npm i -D webpack
npm i -D ts-loader
```

We also install Electron and the accompanying modules that we already examined while creating the Chat application:

```
npm i -D electron
npm i -D electron-debug
npm i -D electron-devtools-installer
```

Finally, we install the React declaration files:

```
npm i -D @types/react
npm i -D @types/react-dom
```

In order to access interfaces of Node.js, we also install the corresponding declarations:

```
npm i -D @types/node
```

Now, we can configure Webpack:

`./webpack.config.js`

```
const path = require( "path" );
module.exports = {
  entry: "./app/ts/index.tsx",
  output: {
    path: path.resolve( __dirname, "./app/build/js/" ),
    filename: "bundle.js"
  },

  target: "electron-renderer",
  devtool: "source-map", // enum
  module: {
    rules: [
      {
        test: /\.tsx?$/,
        use: "ts-loader"
      }
    ]
  }
};
```

Here we set the entry script as `app/ts/index.tsx` and `./app/build/js/bundle.js` as the output. We target Webpack on Electron (`electron-renderer`) and enable source map generation. Finally, we specify a rule, that makes Webpack process any `.ts`/`.tsx` files with the `ts-loader` plugin.

So, if we request a file, such as `require("./path/file.ts")` or `import {member} from "./path/file.ts"`, Webpack will compile it with TypeScript during the bundling. We can make it more convenient using the Webpack option `resolve`:

`./webpack.config.js`

```
{
...
resolve: {
    modules: [
      "node_modules",
      path.resolve(__dirname, "app/ts")
    ],
```

```
    extensions: [ ".ts", ".tsx", ".js"]
  },
  ...
}
```

Here, we state that any encountered module name Webpack tries to resolve against both `node_modules` and `app/ts` directories. So, if we access a module like that, we will have the following:

```
import {member} from "file.ts"
```

According to our configuration, Webpack first checks the existence of `node_modules/file.ts` and then `app/ts/file.ts`. Since we enlisted the `.ts` extension as resolvable, we can omit it from the module name:

```
import {member} from "file"
```

What's left is just configuration for TypeScript:

`tsconfig.json`

```
{
  "compilerOptions": {
    "target": "es6",
    "module": "commonjs",
    "moduleResolution": "node",
    "sourceMap": false,
    "outDir": "../dist/",
    "jsx": "react"
  },

  "files": [
    "./app/ts/index.tsx"
  ]
}
```

It's pretty much the same as we created for the TypeScript introduction examples, except that, here, we do not point the compiler to a directory, but explicitly to the entry script. We also inform the compiler that it shall expect JSX.

React-MDL

Previously, while working on Screen Capturer, we examined the component library Material UI. That's not the only implementation of material design available for React. This time, let's try another one--**React MDL** (`https://react-mdl.github.io/react-mdl/`). So, we install the library and the accompanying declarations:

```
npm i -S react-mdl
npm i -D @types/react-mdl
```

According to the documentation, we enable the library via imports:

```
import "react-mdl/extra/material.css";
import "react-mdl/extra/material.js";
```

Oh! Oh! Webpack won't be able to resolve the CSS module until we configure it accordingly. First, we have to tell Webpack to look for `react-mdl/extra/material.css` and `react-mdl/extra/material.js` in the `node_modules` directory:

```
./webpack.config.js
{
...
resolve: {
    modules: [
        "node_modules",
        path.resolve(__dirname, "app/ts")
    ],
        extensions: [ ".ts", ".tsx", ".js", ".css"]
    },
...
}
```

Second, we add a rule to handle CSS with the `css-loader` plugin:

```
./webpack.config.js
  {
  ...
  module: {
    rules: [
      ...
      {
        test: /\.css$/,
        use: [
            "style-loader",
            "css-loader"
          ]
```

```
        }
    ]
},

    . . .
}
```

Well, now, when meeting `import "react-mdl/extra/material.css"`, Webpack loads the styles and embeds them into the page. But within the CSS content, there are links to a custom `.woff` fonts. We need to make Webpack load the referred font files:

`./webpack.config.js`

```
{
. . .
module: {
    rules: [
        . . .
        {
            test: /\.woff(2)?(\?v=[0-9]\.[0-9]\.[0-9])?$/,
            use: {
                loader: "url-loader",
                options: {
                    limit: 1000000,
                    mimetype: "application/font-woff"
                }
            }
        }
    ]
},

    . . .
}
```

Now, we have to install both the mentioned loaders:

```
npm i -D css-loader
npm i -D style-loader
```

Creating the index.html

The first thing we usually take care of in the Electron application is the main process script that basically creates the application window. For this application, we do not introduce any new concepts about it, so we can reuse `main.js` of the Chat application.

The `index.html` will be very simple:

```
app/index.html
<!DOCTYPE html>
<html lang="en">
    <head>
        <link rel="stylesheet" href="https://fonts.googleapis.com/icon?
        family=Material+Icons">
      <title>RSS Aggregator</title>
  </head>
    <body>
          <div id="root"></div>
          <script src="./build/js/bundle.js"></script>
    </body>
</html>
```

Basically, we load Google's Material Icons font and declare out the bounding element (`div#root`). Of course, we have to load the generated by the Webpack/TypeScipt JavaScript. It is located at `build/js/bundle.js,`, exactly as we configured it in `./webpack.config.js`.

Next, we compose the entry script:

`./app/ts/index.tsx`

```
import "react-mdl/extra/material.css";
import "react-mdl/extra/material.js";

import * as React from "react";
import * as ReactDOM from "react-dom";
import App from "./Containers/App";

ReactDOM.render(
  <App />,
  document.getElementById( "root" )
);
```

As you see, it's similar to what we had in the Screen Capturer static prototype, except for importing React-MDL assets. As for TypeScript, it doesn't really require any changes in the code. Yet, now we definitely have typed interfaces for the module we use (`./node_modules/@types/react-dom/index.d.ts`), meaning if we violate a constraint, for example, of `ReactDOM.render`, we get an error.

Creating the container component

Let's now create the `container` component that we referred to in the entry script:

`./app/ts/Containers/App.tsx`

```
import { Layout, Content } from "react-mdl";
import * as React from "react";

import TitleBar from "../Components/TitleBar";
import Menu from "../Components/Menu";
import Feed from "../Components/Feed";

export default class App extends React.Component<{}, {}> {

  render() {
    return (
      <div className="main-wrapper">
        <Layout fixedHeader fixedDrawer>
          <TitleBar />
          <Menu />
          <Content>
            <Feed />
          </Content>
        </Layout>
      </div>
    );
  }
}
```

Here, we import the components `Layout` and `Content` from the React-MDL library. We use them to layout our custom components `TitleBar`, `Menu`, and `Feed`. According to the React declaration file (`./node_modules/@types/react/index.d.ts`), `React.Component` is a generic type, so we have to provide it with interfaces for the state and props `React.Component<IState, IProps>`. In the static prototype, we have neither states nor props, so we can go with empty types.

Creating the TitleBar component

The next component will represent the title bar:

`./app/ts/Components/TitleBar.tsx`

```
import * as React from "react";
import { remote } from "electron";
```

```
import { Header, Navigation, Icon } from "react-mdl";

export default class TitleBar extends React.Component<{}, {}> {

  private onClose = () => {
    remote.getCurrentWindow().close();
  }
  render() {
    return (
     <Header  scroll>
        <Navigation>
            <a href="#" onClick={this.onClose}><Icon name="close" />
            </a>
        </Navigation>
     </Header>
    );
  }
}
```

Here, we set up the look and feel using the `Header`, `Navigation`, and `Icon` components of React MDL and subscribe for the click event on the close icon. Furthermore, we import the `remote` object of the `electron` module and, by using the `getCurrentWindow` method, we access the current window object. It has the method `close` that we apply to close the window.

Our `Menu` component will contain the list of aggregated feeds. With the buttons `add` and `remove`, users will be able to manage the list. The button `autorenew` serves to update all the feeds.

Creating the Menu component

We are going to keep the feed menu in the `Drawer` component of React MDL that shows up automatically on wide screens and hides in the burger menu on smaller ones:

`./ts/Components/Menu.tsx`

```
import * as React from "react";
import { Drawer, Navigation, Icon, FABButton } from "react-mdl";

export default class Menu extends React.Component<{}, {}> {

  render () {

    return (
     <Drawer  className="mdl-color--blue-grey-900 mdl-
```

```
      color-text--blue-grey-50">
        <Navigation className="mdl-color--blue-grey-80">
          <a>
            <Icon name="& #xE0E5;" />
            Link title
          </a>
        </Navigation>
        <div className="mdl-layout-spacer"></div>
        <div className="tools">
          <FABButton mini>
              <Icon name="add" />
          </FABButton>

          <FABButton mini>
              <Icon name="delete" />
          </FABButton>

          <FABButton mini>
              <Icon name="autorenew" />
          </FABButton>
        </div>
      </Drawer>
    );
  }
}
```

Creating the feed component

Finally, we take care of the main section where we are going display active feed content:

`./app/ts/Components/Feed.tsx`

```
import * as React from "react";
import { Card, CardTitle, CardActions, Button, CardText } from "react-mdl";

export default class Feed extends React.Component<{}, {}> {
  render(){
    return (
      <div className="page-content feed-index">
        <div className="feed-list">

          <Card shadow={0} style={{width: "100%", height: "auto",
          margin: "auto"}}>
            <CardTitle expand style={{color: "#fff", backgroundColor:
            "#46B6AC"}}>
            Title
            </CardTitle>
```

```
            <CardText>
                 Lorem ipsum dolor sit amet, consectetur adipiscing
                 elit. Cras lobortis, mauris quis mollis porta
            </CardText>
            <CardActions border>
                 <Button colored>Open</Button>
            </CardActions>
          </Card>

      </div>

      <div className="feed-contents"></div>
    </div>
  );
 }
}
```

In the `.feed-list` container, we display the list of RSS items, each wrapped with the `Card` component of React MDL. The container `.feed-contents` is a placeholder for the item content.

Everything is ready. We can build and start:

```
npm run build
npm start
```

The output is:

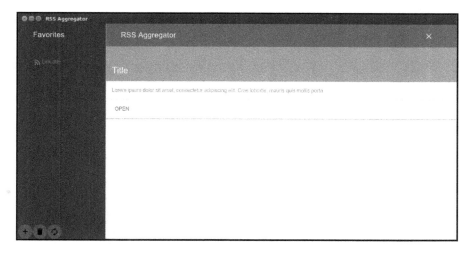

Adding custom styles with SASS

Seemingly, the resulting UI needs additional styling. I suggest that we code our custom styles in SASS:

`./app/sass/app.scss`

```scss
.main-wrapper {
  height: 100vh;
}
```

First of all, we make the top level element (`./app/ts/Containers/App.tsx`) always adapt to the actually window height.

Further, we declare a variable for the fixed height of the title bar and set the layout for feed items and item content containers:

`./app/sass/app.scss`

```scss
$headrHeight: 66px;

.feed-index {
  display: flex;
  flex-flow: row nowrap;
  overflow-y: auto;
  height: calc(100vh - #{$headrHeight});
  &.is-open {
    overflow-y: hidden;
    .feed-list {
      width: 50%;
    }
    .feed-contents {
      width: 50%;
    }
  }
}
.feed-list {
  flex: 1 0 auto;
  width: 100%;
  transition: width 200ms ease;
}
.feed-contents {
  flex: 1 0 auto;
  width: 0;
  transition: width 200ms ease;
}
```

Initially, the width of the feed items container (`.feed-list`) is 100%, while item content one (`.feed-contents`) is hidden (`width:0`). When the parent container (`.feed-index`) receives the new state with the `is-open` class, both the child containers shift to `50%` width gracefully.

Finally, we layout the action buttons in the Menu component:

`./app/sass/app.scss`

```
.tools {
  height: 60px;
  display: flex;
  flex-flow: row nowrap;
  justify-content: space-between;
}
```

Well, we have introduced a new source type (SASS), so we have to adjust the Webpack configuration:

`./webpack.config.js`

```
{
...
resolve: {
  modules: [
      "node_modules",
      path.resolve(__dirname, "app/ts"),
      path.resolve(__dirname, "app/sass")
  ],
      extensions: [ ".ts", ".tsx", ".js", ".scss", ".css"]
},
...
}
```

Now, Webpack accepts `.scss` module names and look for the source in `app/sass`. We also have to configure Webpack to compile SASS in CSS:

`./webpack.config.js`

```
{
...
module: {
  rules: [
    ...
    {
      test: /\.scss$/,
      use: [
```

```
            "style-loader",
            "css-loader",
            "sass-loader"
        ]
    }
  ]
},

...
}
```

Here, we determine that, when resolving the `.scss` file, Webpack uses the `sass-loader` plugin to convert SASS to CSS and then `css-loader` and `style-loader` to load the generated CSS. So, we now have a missing dependency - `sass-loader`; let's install it:

```
npm i -D sass-loader
```

This module relies on the `node-sass` compiler, so we need it also:

```
npm i -D node-sass
```

Why not to check what we get. So we build and start:

```
npm run build
npm start
```

The application looks better now:

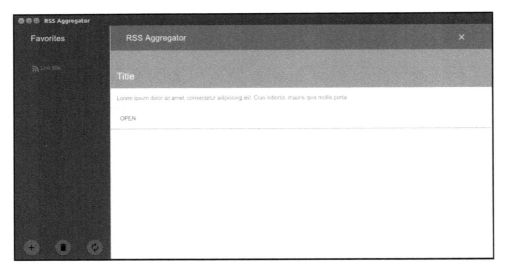

Summary

In this chapter, we dived into TypeScript. We examined basic types in variable declarations and in parameter constraints. We fiddled with interfaces for arrays and plain objects. You learned to interface functions and classes. We took note of abstraction features, such as member accessibility modifiers, parameter property, abstract classes, and methods. You learned to handle group entities with the enum type and string literals. We examined the reuse of interfaces with generic type. We have also seen how to install TypeScript declarations for global libraries and how to write our own when none is available. We started to work on the application. So, we set up Webpack to find and process the `.ts`/`.tsx` modules as well as to load CSS and web fonts. We used components of the React MDL library to create the UI. We extended the Webpack configuration with the SASS loader to process our custom styles. We ended up with a working static prototype.

8
Creating RSS Aggregator with Electron, TypeScript, React, and Redux: Development

In the previous chapter, we embraced TypeScript and came up with a static prototype. Now, we are about unleash the try power of the language. We are going to write application services and cover them with interfaces. We will describe actions and Reducers. On the way, we will examine the creation of Promise-based asynchronous actions and optimistic updates with the `redux-promise` and `redux-actions` modules. We will connect the store to the application and bring the intended functionality to the components. We will also create a simple router and bind it to the store.

Creating a service to fetch RSS

In a nutshell, our application is about reading RSS feeds. So, it would be the right thing to start with the service, which fetches the feed by a given URL and parses it into a structure that we could attach to the applications state. I suggest retrieving the feed XML with the `request` (https://www.npmjs.com/package/request) module and parsing it using the `feedme` module (https://www.npmjs.com/package/feedme). Let's do it first in plain JavaScript. So, we need to install both the packages:

```
npm i -S feedme
npm i -S request
```

We are going to have a function `rss` that uses `request` to fetch feed contents though HTTP(s). This function will accept two arguments: feed URL and a callback function written in a thunk-like manner of Node.js:

```
const request = require( "request" );

function rss( feedUrl, onDone ){
  const feed = {
          title: "",
          items: []
        },
        parser = createFeedParserStream( feed );

  request
    .get( feedUrl )
    .on( "error", ( err ) => {
      onDone( err );
    })
    .on( "end", () => {
      onDone( null, feed );
    })
    .pipe( parser );
}
```

Here, we define the feed data container as a plain object (`feed`). We obtain a Writable Stream (`https://nodejs.org/api/stream.html`) from the not yet written `createFeedParserStream` function and pipe it into the Readable Stream produced by `request` for the specified feed URL. Now, let's add the missing function:

```
const FeedMe = require( "feedme" );

function createFeedParserStream( feed ) {
  const parser = new FeedMe( true );
  parser.on( "title", ( title ) => {
    feed.title = title;
  });
  parser.on( "item", ( item ) => {
    feed.items.push( item );
  });
  return parser;
}
```

Here, we get the stream as the `FeedMe` instance and subscribe for its parsing events. On receiving the feed title, we assign it to `feed.title`. On receiving every item's details, we push them into the `feed.items` array. This function returns the derived parse stream and modifies the `feed` object by the reference passed in with the arguments.

Now, we can consume the `rss` function as follows:

```
rss( "http://feeds.feedburner.com/CssTricks", ( err, feed ) => {
  if ( err ) {
    return console.log( err );
  }
  console.log( feed );
});
```

Despite the fact that, by default, the Node.js core modules still imply long nesting of asynchronous functions, we are quite aware of the undesirable impact known as *Callback Hell*. So, we will convert the service into a Promise:

```
function rss( feedUrl ){
  return new Promise(( resolve, reject ) => {
    const feed = {
            title: "",
            items: []
          },
          parser = createFeedParserStream( feed );

    request
      .get( feedUrl )
      .on( "error", ( err ) => reject( err ) )
      .on( "end", () => resolve( feed ) )
      .pipe( parser );
  });
}
```

Now, it leads to a notably improved development experience:

```
rss( "http://feeds.feedburner.com/CssTricks")
  .then(( feed ) => console.log( feed ) )
  .catch( err => console.log( err ) );
```

Being a Promise, it's also available via the `async/await` syntax:

```
async function handler() {
  try {
    const feed = await rss( "http://feeds.feedburner.com/CssTricks");
  } catch( e ) {
    // handle exception
  }
}

handler();
```

At this point, we can jump back to TypeScript and describe the types that we have in the code. Firstly, we expect the declared `feed` structure to implement the following interface:

`./app/ts/Interfaces/Rss.ts`

```
export interface IRssItem {
  description: string;
  link: string;
  pubdate: string;
  title: string;
}

export interface IFeed {
  title: string;
  items: IRssItem[];
}
```

But wait! The module `feedme` doesn't have a declaration file. It looks like we have to provide it with an interface too. In the previous chapter, I showed a way to introduce a global library into the TypeScript scope by using triple-slash directives and ambient declarations. That's not the only possible solution. We can declare the interface in a module:

`./app/ts/Services/IFeedMe.ts`

```
import { IRssItem } from "../Interfaces/Rss";
export interface IFeedMe {
  new ( flag?: boolean ): NodeJS.WritableStream;
  on( event: "title", onTitle: ( title: string ) => void): void;
  on( event: "item", onItem: ( item: IRssItem ) => void ): void;
}
```

In the service, we import the `IFeedMe` interface and assign the `feedme` export to a constant of type `IFeedMe`:

```
import { IFeedMe } from "./IFeedMe";
const FeedMe: IFeedMe = require( "feedme" );
```

After rewriting our service in TypeScript, its source will look as follows:

`/app/ts/Services/rss.ts`

```
import { IRssItem, IFeed } from "../Interfaces/Rss";
import { IFeedMe } from "./IFeedMe";
import * as request from "request";
const FeedMe: IFeedMe = require( "feedme" );

function createFeedParserStream( feed: IFeed ): NodeJS.WritableStream {
  const parser = new FeedMe( true );
```

```
    parser.on( "title", ( title: string ) => {
      feed.title = title;
    });
    parser.on( "item", ( item: IRssItem ) => {
      feed.items.push( item );
    });
    return parser;
  }


  export default function rss( feedUrl: string ): Promise<IFeed> {
    const feed: IFeed = {
          title: "",
          items: []
        };
    return new Promise<IFeed>(( resolve, reject ) => {
      request.get( feedUrl )
        .on( "error", ( err: Error ) => {
          reject( err );
        })
        .on( "end", () => {
          resolve( feed );
        })
        .pipe( createFeedParserStream( feed ) );
    });
  }
```

What is changed? We regarded the export `feedme` module with an interface (`FeedMe:`
`IFeedMe`). We defined the contract for the `createFeedParserStream` function. It accepts
the `IFeed` type as input and returns `NodeJS.WritableStream`. We did the same for the
service function `rss`. It expects a string and returns a Promise, which resolves in the `IFeed`
type.

Creating a service to manage feed menu

Well, now we can fetch RSS feeds. But the plan was to have a manageable menu of feeds. I
think, we can represent the menu in an array of items, where each item can be described
with the following interface:

`./app/ts/Interfaces/index.ts`

```
  export interface IMenuItem {
    url: string;
```

```
      title: string;
      id: string;
    }
```

As for the service itself, let's also start with the interface:

`./app/ts/Services/IMenu.ts`

```
    import { IMenuItem } from "../Interfaces";

    export interface IMenu {
      items: IMenuItem[];
      clear(): void;
      remove( url: string ): IMenuItem[];
      add( url: string, title: string ): IMenuItem[];
      load(): IMenuItem[];
    }
```

To some degree, it's like Test-Driven development. We describe the contents of the class without implementation to get the whole picture. Then, we populate the members one by one:

`./app/ts/Services/Menu.ts`

```
    import sha1 = require( "sha1" );
    import { IMenu } from "./IMenu";
    import { IMenuItem } from "../Interfaces";


    class Menu implements IMenu {

      items: IMenuItem[] = [];

      constructor( private ns: string ){
      }

      clear(): void {
        this.items =  [];
        this.save();
      }

      remove( url: string ): IMenuItem[] {
        this.items =  this.items.filter(( item ) => item.url !== url );
        this.save();
        return this.items;
      }

      add( url: string, title: string ): IMenuItem[] {
```

```
        const id = <string> sha1( url );
        this.items.push({ id, url, title });
        this.save();
        return this.items;
    }

    private save(): void {
        localStorage.setItem( this.ns, JSON.stringify( this.items ) );
    }

    load(): IMenuItem[] {
        this.items = JSON.parse( localStorage.getItem( this.ns ) || "[]" );
        return this.items;
    }
}

export default Menu;
```

What is going on here? Firstly, we import the `sha1` module
(`https://www.npmjs.com/package/sha1`) that we are going to use to calculate SHA1 hash
(`https://en.wikipedia.org/wiki/SHA-1`) of a feed URL. That's an external module, which
resolves to a non-module entity and, therefore, cannot be imported using the ES6 syntax.
That's why, we go with the `require` function. But we still want TypeScript to consider the
module declaration file (`@types/sha1`), so we declare its container as `import sha1`. We
also import, in the module scope, the service interface (`IMenu`) and menu item type
(`IMenuItem`). Our constructor accepts namespace as a string. By prefixing the parameter
with an accessibility modifier, we declare the `ns` property and assign the parameter's value
to it. The instance of `Menu` will keep the actual menu state in the property `items`. Private
method `save` stores the value of the `items` property to `localStorage`. All the three `add`,
`remove`, and `clear` methods modify the `this.items` array and synchronize with
`localStorage` by using the save method. Finally, the method load updates `this.item`
with the array stored in `localStorage`.

Actions and Reducers

So, we have our core services and can start designing the Redux store. We can describe the intended state mutations in a table:

Action creator	Action Type	State Impact
toggleOpenAddFeed	TOGGLE_ADD_FEED	state.isOpenAddFeed
addFeed	ADD_FEED	state.isOpenAddFeed state.feedError state.items
setFeedError	SET_FEED_ERROR	state.feedError
removeFeed	REMOVE_FEED	state.feedError
fetchFeed	FETCH_FEED	state.items state.feedError
fetchMenu	FETCH_MENU	state.menu state.items state.activeFeedUrl
setActiveFeed	SET_ACTIVE_FEED	state.activeFeedUrl

First of all, we need to populate our feed menu. For that, we are going to have a modal window with a form to add a feed. The action creator function toggleOpenAddFeed will be used to toggle the visibility of the modal window.

When the form in the modal window is submitted, the component will call the addFeed function. The function fetches the feed by the supplied URL, obtains its title, and appends the menu with a new item. As it involves user input and network operations, we have to cover the failure scenario. So, we introduce the setFeedError function that sets a message in the application state. When we update the menu, the corresponding service synchronizes the change with localStorage. That means we need an action to read the menu. The function fetchMenu will take care of it. Besides, it will utilize the rss service to fetch the items of all the feeds in the menu in an aggregative list. What's more, we are going to provide the option to navigate through the menu. When a user clicks on an item, the component calls setActiveFeed to mark the item as active and the function fetchFeed to update the Feed component with the items of the selected feed.

When working on action creator functions, we declare the types and use them as references from the Reducers. That means we need a module with a bunch of constants representing action types:

`./app/ts/Constants/index.ts`

```
export const TOGGLE_ADD_FEED = "TOGGLE_ADD_FEED";
export const SET_ACTIVE_FEED = "SET_ACTIVE_FEED";
export const FETCH_MENU = "FETCH_MENU";
export const ADD_FEED = "ADD_FEED";
export const SET_ADD_FEED_ERROR = "SET_ADD_FEED_ERROR";
export const SET_FEED_ERROR = "SET_FEED_ERROR";
export const FETCH_FEED = "FETCH_FEED";
export const REMOVE_FEED = "REMOVE_FEED";
```

Since we are here, let's also define a few configuration constants:

```
export const MENU_STORAGE_NS = "rssItems";
export const FEED_ITEM_PER_PAGE = 10;
```

The first (`MENU_STORAGE_NS`) specifies the namespace that we are going to use in `localStorage` for the menu. The second (`FEED_ITEM_PER_PAGE`) determines how many items we display per page. That applies for both a selected feed and aggregative one.

In `Chapter 5`, *Creating a Screen Capturer with NW.js, React, and Redux: Planning, Design, and Development,* we used the third-party module `redux-act` to abstract the creation of actions and Reducers. It was really handy, but it doesn't fit if you need asynchronous actions. So, this time, we are going to use the `redux-actions` module (`https://github.com/acdlite/redux-actions`) instead. Let's check what that is on a JavaScript example. First, we create a synchronous action by calling the `createAction` function of `redux-actions`:

```
import { createAction } from "redux-actions";
const toggleOpenAddFeed = createAction( "TOGGLE_ADD_FEED", ( toggle ) =>
toggle );
```

So far, it looks pretty much similar to the syntax of `redux-act`. We can run the newly created function:

```
console.log( toggleOpenAddFeed( true ) ),
```

We then get an action object with a mandatory `type` property and a multipurpose `payload` one:

```
{ payload: "TOGGLE_ADD_FEED", type: true }
```

Now, we can make a Reducer by using the `handleActions` function of `redux-actions`:

```
import { handleActions } from "redux-actions";
const app = handleActions({

  "TOGGLE_ADD_FEED": ( state, action ) => ({
    ...state, isOpenAddFeed: action.payload
  })

}, defaultState );
```

The function `handleActions` expects a plain object that maps handlers to actions using the action type as a reference. Every handler callback takes in the latest state object and the dispatched action--the same as the canonical Reducer (`http://redux.js.org/docs/basics/Reducers.html`).

But what about asynchronous actions? For example, we are going use the `rss` services for fetching feeds. The service returns a Promise. Thanks to `redux-actions`, we can create an action as simple as the following:

```
const fetchFeed = createAction( "FETCH_FEED", async ( url: string ) =>
await rss( url ) );
```

Isn't it beautiful? We just pass, for the handler, an asynchronous function. The action will be dispatched as soon as the Promise of the handler resolves:

```
const app = handleActions({
  "FETCH_FEED": ( state, action ) => (
      ...state,
      items: action.payload.items
  })

}, defaultState );
```

Hold on! But what if the Promise gets rejected? The module `redux-actions` relies on optimistic updates. In the case of failure, incoming action acquires an extra property `error` when we can find an error message:

```
const app = handleActions({

  "FETCH_FEED": ( state, action ) => ({
    if ( action.error ) {
      return { ...state, feedError: `Cannot fetch feed: ${action.payload}`
};
    }
      return {
        ...state,
```

```
        items: action.payload.items
    };
  })

}, defaultState );
```

Now after considering how we are going to implement action creators and Reducers, we can cover the store assets with interfaces. First, we declare the interface for the state:

```
./app/ts/Interfaces/index.ts
```

```
//...
export interface IAppState {
  isOpenAddFeed: boolean;
  menu: IMenuItem[];
  items: IRssItem[];
  feedError: string;
  activeFeedUrl: string;
}
```

The property isOpenAddFeed is a boolean determining if the modal window with the form for adding a new feed is visible. The property menu contains the list of menu items and is used in the Menu component to build the menu. The property items consists of RSS items and is used to build the list in the Feed component. The property feedError stores the last error message and activeFeedUrl keeps the last requested feed URL.

Next, we describe the actions:

```
import { Action } from "redux-actions";

export interface IAppActions {
  toggleOpenAddFeed: ( toggle: boolean ) => Action<boolean>;
  setActiveFeed:  ( url: string ) => Action<string>;
  setFeedError: ( msg: string ) => Action<string>;
  fetchMenu: () => Promise<IMenuRssPayload>;
  addFeed: ( url: string ) => Promise<IMenuItem[]>;
  removeFeed: ( url: string ) => Promise<IMenuItem[]>;
  fetchFeed: ( url: string ) => Promise<IFeed>;
}
```

The module redux-actions exports though the declaration file Action type. So, we state that the functions toggleOpenAddFeed, setActiveFeed, and setFeedError return plain objects that confront the Action type constraints. In other words, in addition to the type property, those may have payload and error. Action is a generic type, so we clarify what type is expected in payload, for example, Action<boolean> means { type: string, payload: boolean }.

Asynchronous actions `fetchMenu`, `addFeed`, `removeFeed`, and `fetchFeed` return Promises. Again, we specify explicitly what type is expected when a Promise resolves. Speaking of which, the function `fetchMenu` refers to the missing `IMenuRssPayload` type. Let's add it:

`./app/ts/Interfaces/index.ts`

```
export interface IMenuRssPayload {
  menuItems: IMenuItem[];
  rssItems: IRssItem[];
}
```

The function resolves with an object containing both menu items and RSS items of the aggregative list.

It seems like we are ready to implement the store. So, we will start with actions:

`./app/ts/Actions/actions.ts`

```
import { createAction } from "redux-actions";
import * as vo from "../Constants";
import { IMenuItem, IRssItem, IFeed, IMenuRssPayload } from
"../Interfaces";
import Menu from "../Services/Menu";
import rss from "../Services/rss";
const menu = new Menu( vo.MENU_STORAGE_NS );
```

First, we import `createAction`, the earlier defined constants and interfaces, and both the services such as `rss` and `Menu` constructor. We create an instance of the menu in the namespace imported from the configuration constants. Next, we add synchronous actions:

```
const feedActions = {

  toggleOpenAddFeed: createAction<boolean, boolean>(
    vo.TOGGLE_ADD_FEED, ( toggle: boolean ) => toggle
  ),

  setActiveFeed: createAction<string, string>(
    vo.SET_ACTIVE_FEED, ( url: string ) => url
  ),

  setFeedError: createAction<string, string>(
    vo.SET_FEED_ERROR, ( msg: string ) => msg
  ),

  removeFeed: createAction<IMenuItem[], string>(
```

```
      vo.REMOVE_FEED, ( url: string ) => menu.remove( url )
   ),
};
```

Here, we use the pattern we examined earlier in the JavaScript example for `createAction`. The only difference is that `createAction` is a generic type in the TypeScript scope, so we have to specify what type the action creator will pass in the `payload` property and what it expects with the first parameter. All of these functions take in a single argument. If we needed more, we would express it as `createAction<Payload, Arg1, Arg2>` or even `createAction<Payload, Arg1, Arg2, Arg3, Arg4>`.

Now, we extend `feedActions` with asynchronous actions:

```
const feedActions = {
  //...

  fetchFeed: createAction<Promise<IFeed>, string>(
    vo.FETCH_FEED, async ( url: string ) => await rss( url )
  ),

  addFeed: createAction<Promise<IMenuItem[]>, string>(
    vo.ADD_FEED,
    async ( url: string ) => {
      if ( menu.items.find( item => item.url === url ) ) {
        throw new Error( "This feed is already in the list" );
      }
      const feed = await rss( url );
      if ( !feed.title ) {
        throw new Error( "Unsupported format" );
      }
      return menu.add( url, feed.title );
    }
  ),

  fetchMenu: createAction<Promise<IMenuRssPayload>>(
    vo.FETCH_MENU, async () => {
      menu.load();
      let promises = menu.items.map( item => rss( item.url ) );
      return Promise.all( promises )
        .then(( feeds: IFeed[] ) => {
          if ( !feeds.length ) {
            return { menuItems: [], rssItems: [] };
          }
          let all = feeds
              .map( feed => feed.items )
              // combine [[items],[item]] in a flat array
              .reduce(( acc: IRssItem[], items: IRssItem[] ) =>
```

```
                    acc.concat( items ) )
                    // sort the list by publication date DESC
                    .sort(( a, b ) => {
                      let aDate = new Date( a.pubdate ),
                          bDate = new Date( b.pubdate );
                      return bDate.getTime() - aDate.getTime();
                    })
                    .slice( 0, vo.FEED_ITEM_PER_PAGE );
                return { menuItems: menu.items, rssItems: all };
            });
        }
    )
};

    export default feedActions;
```

The function `fetchFeed` simply delegates the Promise of the `rss` service. The function `addFeed` first checks whether a given URL already exists in the menu. If `true`, it throws an exception. Then, the function obtains the feed from the `rss` service and adds the item into the menu. Finally, `fetchMenu` performs a number of tasks. It reloads the menu from `localStorage`. That is exactly what one may expect of the action. But I want the function to generate the aggregative list as well. So, it collects the Promises of the `rss` service for every feed available in the menu. It applies `Promise.all` to resolve the collected set of Promises. The method results in the list of feeds. We need to combine all the items in a flat array, sort it by publication date, and limit it to the number we set in the `FEED_ITEM_PER_PAGE` constant.

Now, we start on the Reducer:

`./app/ts/Reducers/app.ts`

```
    import { handleActions, Action } from "redux-actions";
    import { IAppState, IMenuRssPayload } from "../Interfaces";
    import * as vo from "../Constants";

    const defaultState: IAppState = {
      isOpenAddFeed: false,
      menu: [],
      items: [],
      feedError: "",
      activeFeedUrl: ""
    };
```

Here, we imported the `handleActions` function and the `Action` interface, and from `redux-actions`, our interfaces and constants. We also defined the default state for the Reducer.

Next, we create the Reducer:

```
const app = handleActions<IAppState>({

  [ vo.TOGGLE_ADD_FEED ]: ( state, action ) => ({
    ...state, isOpenAddFeed: action.payload
  }),

  [ vo.ADD_FEED ]: ( state, action ) => {
    if ( action.error ) {
      return { ...state, feedError: `Cannot add feed:
      ${action.payload}` };
    }
    return { ...state, feedError: "", isOpenAddFeed: false, menu:
    action.payload };
  },

  [ vo.SET_FEED_ERROR ]: ( state, action ) => ({
    ...state, feedError: action.payload
  }),

  [ vo.REMOVE_FEED ]: ( state, action ) => {
    if ( action.error ) {
      return { ...state, feedError: `Cannot remove feed:
      ${action.payload}` };
    }
    return { ...state, menu: action.payload };
  },


  [ vo.FETCH_MENU ]: ( state, action: Action<IMenuRssPayload> ) => {
    if ( action.error ) {
      return { ...state, feedError: `Cannot fetch menu:
      ${action.payload}` };
    }
    return {
      ...state,
      menu: action.payload.menuItems,
      items: action.payload.rssItems,
      activeFeedUrl: ""
    };
  },

  [ vo.FETCH_FEED ]: ( state, action ) => {
    if ( action.error ) {
      return { ...state, feedError: `Cannot fetch feed:
      ${action.payload}` };
    }
```

```
        return {
          ...state,
          items: action.payload.items
        };
      },

      [ vo.SET_ACTIVE_FEED ]: ( state, action ) => ({
        ...state, activeFeedUrl: action.payload
      })


    }, defaultState );

    export default app;
```

`handleActions` is generic type, so we can specify the constraints for the `state` object it operates with. In the supplied object, we describe how every dispatched action shall modify the state. Thus, `toggleOpenAddFeed` (`TOGGLE_ADD_FEED`) toggles the `isOpenAddFeed` property. The function `addFeed` (`ADD_FEED`), in case of success, populates the `menu` property from the action payload and, besides, resets `feedError` and `isOpenAddFeed`. If the Promise was rejected, it sets `feedError` with an error message. The function `setFeedError` (`SET_FEED_ERROR`) simply sets `feedError` from the action payload. The function `removeFeed` (`REMOVE_FEED`) updates the menu, so here, it populates the `menu` state property with the updated list. The function `fetchFeed` (`FETCH_FEED`) updates the `items` property with just the fetched feed items. The function `fetchMenu` (`FETCH_MENU`) reloads the menu and generates the aggregative list, so it updates both `menu` and (RSS) `items`. Finally, the function `setActiveFeed` (`SET_ACTIVE_FEED`) simply saves the selected item URL in the state.

In a large scalable application, we use multiple Reducers combined together with the `combineReducers` function of `redux`. For this little application, only the Reducer will be sufficient. Yet, I suggest, we follow the practice:

`./app/ts/Reducers/index.ts`

```
    import { combineReducers } from "redux";
    import app from "./app";

    const reducer = combineReducers({ state: app });
    export default reducer;
```

This changes our state tree. So, the top level state object can be described now with the following interface:

`./app/ts/Interfaces/index.ts`

```
export interface IRootState {
  state: IAppState;
}
```

Connecting to the store

We have action creators and we have Reducers and, now, we are about to make them available across the application. As you can remember from Chapter 5, *Creating a Screen Capturer with NW.js, React, and Redux: Planning, Design, and Development*, the module redux provides the function createStore, which takes in combined reducers to produce the store. The module react-redux exports the provider higher-order component that accepts the store with the props and makes it available through connect across the inner component tree. The function createStore accepts middleware that is combined with the compose function of redux. As we already discussed in this application, we need asynchronous actions. Here, we can use the redux-thunk (https://www.npmjs.com/package/redux-thunk) middleware that allows us to write action creators, which return functions instead of plain objects. These functions take in references to the dispatch and getState functions as parameters. So, we can dispatch deferred actions. For example, we need to read the RSS feed by URL, so we reflect it on the application state with the following action creator:

```
function fetchFeedAsync( url ) {
  return dispatch => {
    dispatch( fetchFeedRequest() );
    rss( url )
      .then( data => dispatch( fetchFeedSuccess( data ) ))
      .catch( e  => dispatch( fetchFeedFailure( e ) ));
  };
}
```

Before making asynchronous HTTP request for the feed contents, we dispatch fetchFeedRequest and, when the request is resolved, fetchFeedSuccess or fetchFeedFailure if it was rejected.

It is all nice, but is too verbose. Just to get the data retrieved through HTTP, we write four (!) action creators. Instead we can follow an optimistic updates approach and go with a single action creator. That involves an additional middleware `redux-promise` (https://www.npmjs.com/package/redux-promise), which plays nicely with `redux-actions`:

```
const fetchFeed = createAction(
    "FETCH_FEED", async ( url ) => await rss( url )
  )
```

Now, when combining all together, we come up with the following update for the entry script:

`./app/ts/index.tsx`

```
import { Provider } from "react-redux";
import { createStore, applyMiddleware, compose } from "redux";
import thunkMiddleware from "redux-thunk";
import * as promiseMiddleware from "redux-promise";

const storeEnhancer = compose(
  applyMiddleware(
    thunkMiddleware,
    promiseMiddleware
  )
);

const store = createStore(
  appReducers,   storeEnhancer
);

ReactDOM.render(
  <Provider store={store}>
      <App {...this.props} />
  </Provider>,
  document.getElementById( "root" )
);
```

In the container component, we need to add two functions that inform `connect` of how we want to map state and action creators to the component props:

`./app/ts/Containers/App.tsx`

```
// mapping state to the props
const mapStateToProps = ( state: IRootState ) => state;

import actions from "../Actions/actions";
```

```
// mapping actions to the props
const mapDispatchToProps = {
  ...actions
};
```

Here, we have mapped the state to the props simply one to one. As we have the store expressed as `{ state: applicationStateTree }`, we receive, in the props, an extra property `state` pointing at the actual state tree. As for the action creators, we destructure the namespace and attach every available function as a new property to the props. So the props of the container components can now be described with the following type:

`./app/ts/Interfaces/index.ts`

```
export type TStore = IRootState & IAppActions;
```

We shall refer to the props with this type in the `React.Component` generic.

We pass the container component's properties downward by destructuring `store={this.props}`. Thus, every child component receives an object of the `TStore` type with the property store:

```
class App extends React.Component<TStore, {}> {
  render() {
    return (
      <div className="main-wrapper">
        <ErrorAlert store={this.props} />
        <Layout fixedHeader fixedDrawer>
          <TitleBar />
          <Menu store={this.props} />
          <Content>
            <Feed store={this.props} />
          </Content>
        </Layout>
      </div>
    );
  }
}

// connect store to App
export default connect(
  mapStateToProps,
  mapDispatchToProps
)( App );
```

Personally, I find the container to be a good place for bootstrap logic. In particular, I would like the load menu from `localStorage` in the start of the application. Actually, it can be done straight after the container component is mounted:

```
class App extends React.Component<TStore, {}> {

  componentDidMount() {
    this.props.fetchMenu();
  }
}
```

So, we call the `fetchMenu` action creator, which is now available in the props. This dispatches the action, the Reducer modifies the state and any component, and all the components reflect the state change.

Consuming store from the components

If you were attentive enough, you didn't miss that, in container's JSX, we introduced a new component `ErrorAlert`. Since we have an error state (`state.feedError`), we need to visualize it:

`./app/ts/Components/ErrorAlert.tsx`

```
import * as React from "react";
import { Dialog, DialogTitle,
  DialogContent, DialogActions, Button } from "react-mdl";
import { TStore } from "../Interfaces";

interface IProps {
  store: TStore;
}

export default class ErrorAlert extends React.Component<IProps, {}> {

  private onClose = () => {
    this.props.store.setFeedError( "" );
  }

  render() {
    const { feedError } = this.props.store.state;
    return (
    <Dialog open={Boolean(feedError)}>
          <DialogTitle>Houston, we have a problem</DialogTitle>
          <DialogContent>
            <p>{feedError}</p>
```

```
        </DialogContent>
        <DialogActions>
          <Button type="button" onClick={this.onClose}>Close</Button>
        </DialogActions>
      </Dialog>
    );
  }
}
```

By using `Dialog` and related components of the React MDL library, we describe a modal window, which shows up when `state.feedError` is not empty. The window has a button `Close`, which has a handler `onClose` subscribed for the click event. The handler calls the `setFeedError` action to reset `state.feedError`:

We can now modify the `Menu` components to display and manage the RSS menu from the state:

`./app/ts/Components/Menu.tsx`

```
import * as React from "react";

import { Drawer, Navigation, Icon, FABButton } from "react-mdl";
import { IMenuItem, TStore } from "../Interfaces";
import AddFeedDialog from "./AddFeedDialog";

interface IProps {
  store: TStore;
}
```

```
export default class Menu extends React.Component<IProps, {}> {

  static makeClassName = ( toggle: boolean ) => {
    const classList = [ "mdl-navigation__link" ];
    toggle && classList.push( "mdl-navigation__link--current" );
    return classList.join( " " );
  }

  private onAddFeed = () => {
    this.props.store.toggleOpenAddFeed( true );
  }

  private onRemoveFeed = () => {
    const { removeFeed, fetchMenu, state } = this.props.store;
    removeFeed( state.activeFeedUrl );
    fetchMenu();
  }

  private onRefresh = () => {
    this.props.store.fetchMenu();
  }

  render (){
    const { state } = this.props.store,
          menu = state.menu || [];

    return (
      <Drawer  className="mdl-color--blue-grey-900 mdl-
      color-text--blue-grey-50">
        <AddFeedDialog store={this.props.store} />
        <Navigation className="mdl-color--blue-grey-80">

        { menu.map(( item: IMenuItem ) => (
          <a key={item.id} href={`#${item.id}`}
          className={Menu.makeClassName( item.url ===
          state.activeFeedUrl )}>
           <Icon name="& #xE0E5;" />
           {item.title}
          </a>
        )) }
        </Navigation>
        <div className="mdl-layout-spacer"></div>
        <div className="tools">
          <FABButton mini onClick={this.onAddFeed}>
              <Icon name="add" />
          </FABButton>
          { state.activeFeedUrl && (
          <FABButton mini>
```

```
            <Icon name="delete" onClick={this.onRemoveFeed} />
        </FABButton>
        )}
        <FABButton mini onClick={this.onRefresh}>
            <Icon name="autorenew" />
        </FABButton>
      </div>
    </Drawer>
  );
  }
}
```

Here, we take `state.menu` from the property `store` and map it to build the list of menu items. We represent items as links with `item.title` as contents and `item.id` (sha1 of URL) in `href`. We use the static method `makeClassName` to build the item `className`. It will be `"mdl-navigation__link"` normally and `"mdl-navigation__link mdl-navigation__link--current"` when the item is an active one. We also subscribe to the handlers for click events on the Add, Remove, and Refresh (Autorenew icon) buttons. The first one calls the `toggleOpenAddFeed` action with `true` to display the modal window for adding a feed. The second uses the `removeFeed` action with `activeFeedUrl` from the state. It also calls the `fetchMenu` action to refresh the aggregative list. The last one simply calls the `fetchMenu` action.

Now, we have to create a component representing the modal window with the form to add a feed:

`./app/ts/Components/AddFeedDialog.tsx`

```
import { Button, Dialog, DialogTitle, DialogContent, DialogActions,
Textfield } from "react-mdl";
import * as React from "react";
import { TStore } from "../Interfaces";

interface IProps {
  store: TStore;
}
export default class AddFeedDialog extends React.Component<IProps, {}> {

  private urlEl: Textfield;
  private formEl: HTMLFormElement;
  private onSubmit = ( e: React.MouseEvent<HTMLFormElement> ) => {
    // https://github.com/react-mdl/react-mdl/issues/465
    const urlEl = this.urlEl as any;
    e.preventDefault();
    this.save( urlEl.inputRef.value );
  }
```

```
async save( url: string ){
  const { addFeed, fetchMenu } = this.props.store;
  await addFeed( url );
  await fetchMenu();
  if ( !this.props.store.state.feedError ){
    this.formEl.reset();
  }
}
private close = () => {
  this.props.store.toggleOpenAddFeed( false );
  this.formEl.reset();
}

render() {
  const { isOpenAddFeed } = this.props.store.state;

  return (
    <div>

      <Dialog open={isOpenAddFeed}>
        <DialogTitle>New Feed</DialogTitle>
        <DialogContent>
          <form onSubmit={this.onSubmit} ref={(el: HTMLFormElement)
          => { this.formEl = el; }}>

          <Textfield
              label="URL"
              required
              floatingLabel
              ref={(el: Textfield) => { this.urlEl = el; }}
          />

          </form>
        </DialogContent>
        <DialogActions>
          <Button type="button" onClick={this.onSubmit}>Save</Button>
          <Button type="button" onClick={this.close}>Cancel</Button>
        </DialogActions>
      </Dialog>
    </div>
  );
}
}
```

Similar to `ErrorAlert`, we use `Dialog` and the related components of React MDL to render the modal window. The window has a form and an input represented with the `Textfield` component of React MDL. We make both elements available in the instance scope by using the `ref` attribute. We subscribe the `onSubmit` method for the form `submit` event. In the handler, we take the value from the input field by the reference (`Textfield` is referenced as `this.urlEl`; thus, internal input can be accessed as `this.urlEl.inputRef` according to React MDL API) and pass it to the private method `save`. The `save` method calls `addFeed` and `fetchMenu` to update the aggregative list. The window also includes the `Close` button, which invokes the `toggleOpenAddFeed` action with false on a click event.

That's left just to update the `Feed` component:

`./app/ts/Components/Feed.tsx`

```
import * as React from "react";
import { shell } from "electron";

import { Card, CardTitle, CardActions, Button, CardText } from "react-mdl";
import { IRssItem, TStore } from "../Interfaces";

interface IProps {
  store: TStore;
}

export default class Feed extends React.Component<IProps, {}> {

  private indexEl: HTMLElement;
  private contentsEl: HTMLElement;
  private webviewEl: Electron.WebviewTag;

  // Convert HTML into plain text
  static stripHtml( html: string ){
    var tmp = document.createElement( "DIV" );
    tmp.innerHTML = html;
    return tmp.textContent || tmp.innerText || "";
  }

  private onCloseLink = () => {
    this.indexEl.classList.remove( "is-open" );
    this.webviewEl.src = "blank";
  }

  private onOpenLink = ( e: React.MouseEvent<HTMLElement> ) => {
    const btn = e.target as HTMLElement,
          url = btn.dataset[ "link" ];
    e.preventDefault();
```

```
        this.indexEl.classList.add( "is-open" );
        this.webviewEl.src = url;
    }

    componentDidMount() {
        this.webviewEl = this.contentsEl.firstChild as Electron.WebviewTag;
        this.webviewEl.addEventListener( "new-window", ( e ) => {
            e.preventDefault();
            shell.openExternal( e.url );
        });
    }

    render(){
        const { items } = this.props.store.state;
        return (
            <div className="page-content feed-index" ref={(el: HTMLElement)
            => { this.indexEl = el; }}>
                <div className="feed-list">

                { items.map(( item: IRssItem, inx: number ) => (
                    <Card key={inx} shadow={0} style={{width: "100%", height:
                    "auto", margin: "auto"}}>
                        <CardTitle expand style={{color: "#fff", backgroundColor:
                        "#46B6AC"}}>
                        {item.title}
                        </CardTitle>
                            <CardText onClick={this.onCloseLink}>
                                { item.description ? Feed.stripHtml( item.description )
                            : "" }
                            </CardText>
                            <CardActions border>
                                <Button colored data-link={item.link} onClick=
                                {this.onOpenLink}>Open</Button>
                            </CardActions>
                    </Card>
                )) }
                </div>
                <div className="feed-contents"
                    ref={(el: HTMLElement) => { this.contentsEl = el; }}
                    dangerouslySetInnerHTML={{
                    __html: `<webview class="feed-contents__src"></webview>`
                }}></div>
            </div>
        );
    }
}
```

Here, we map `state.items` to render RSS items, while we use the `stripHtml` static method to sanitize item description. Every item is provided with the `Open` button that has a subscriber `onOpenLink`. This method makes visible, the `.feed-contents` column and changes the `src` attribute of `WebView`. This causes `WebView` to load the feed item URL. Why do we use `WebView` and not iFrame? Because `WebView` is the intended container for guest contents in both Electron and NW.js (`https://electron.atom.io/docs/api/webview-tag/`). `WebView` runs in a separate process and it doesn't have the same permission as your page. So, it's supposed to prevent third-party pages, and scripts that are affecting and harmful to your application.

We could not reference `WebView` directly because JSX doesn't have such an element and we had to inject it. So, we use the `componentDidMount` life-cycle method to reach it via DOM. What is more, we subscribe to the `new-window` event, which happens when the page loaded within `WebView` tries to open a new window/tab. We prevent that from happening, but open the requested page in the external browser instead.

Chin-chin! It's a working application now. So, we can build it:

```
npm build
```

And we can run:

```
npm start
```

The output will be:

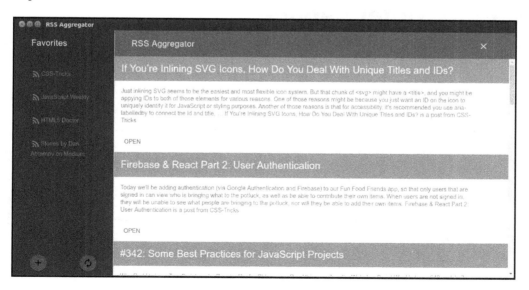

If we hit "open" link on any of RSS items the content panel slides in and it loads the corresponding contents into the WebView:

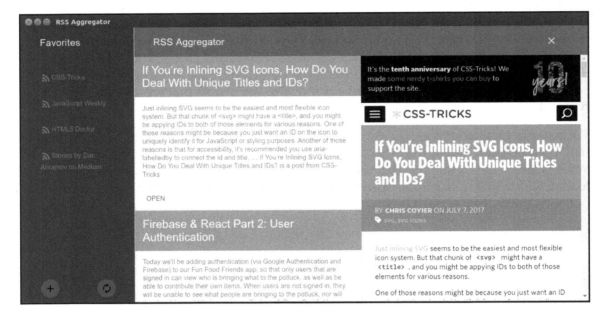

Creating router service

Everything is fine, except we cannot really select a feed from the menu. We have the state property `activeFeedUrl`, which is already considered by the Menu component, but we have never used the `setActiveFeed` action so far to set this state. Nonetheless, in the Menu component, we provided all the items with hash links. To serve browser location navigation, we need a router. There are many implementations available as installable modules. Yet, in this simple example, we will create our own:

`./app/ts/Services/Router.ts`

```
import * as Redux from "redux";
import { IRootState, IMenuItem } from "../Interfaces";
import actions from "../Actions/actions";

export default class Router {

  constructor( private store: Redux.Store<IRootState> ) {
  }
```

```
getFeedUrlById( id: string ): string {
  const { state } = this.store.getState(),
        match = state.menu.find(( item: IMenuItem ) =>  item.id ===
        id );
    return match ? match.url : "";
}

register(){
  window.addEventListener( "hashchange", () => {
    const url =  this.getFeedUrlById( window.location.hash.substr( 1 ) );
    this.store.dispatch( actions.setActiveFeed( url ) );
    url && this.store.dispatch( actions.fetchFeed( url ) );
  });
}

}
```

On the construction, the service takes in the store instance and assigns it to the private property `store`. With the `register` method, we subscribe to the document `hashchange` event, which triggers every time the `location.hash` changes. It happens, for example, when we request from the address bar something like `#some-id`. In the handler function, we extract SHA1 from `location.hash` (everything what follows # symbol) and use the `getFeedUrlById` method to find the associated feed URL (we provide items with IDs in the `add` method of the `Menu` service). As we have the URL, we dispatch the `setActiveFeed` action to set the `activeFeedUrl` state property. In addition, we dispatch `fetchFeed` to fetch the selected feed.

We can now enable the service in entry script as follows:

`./app/ts/index.tsx`

```
const router = new Router( store );
router.register();
```

Summary

We started this chapter by implementing the `rss` service. We used the `request` module to fetch feed contents. We obtained a Writable Stream from the `feedme` module and configured it to parse the input into our feed container object. We piped the `feedme` parser into the Readable Stream produced by `request`. The module `feedme` was missing the declaration file, so we provided it with an interface.

Then, we created the `Menu` service, which can be used to manage and persist the menu of feeds. We considered actions and state structure required by the application. We applied the `redux-actions` module for creating actions and the Reducer. On the way, we examined the optimistic updates approach. While creating the store, we practiced two store enhancers `redux-thunk` and `redux-promise` that help to deal with asynchronous actions. We connected our existing components to the store and modified them accordingly. Besides this, we have written two new components, both utilizing the `Dialog` component of React MDL library. The first one displays an application error if it occurs. The second shows and handles the feed adding form. Among other things, we made the `Feed` component to load the feed item URL on demand. So, you learned to use the `WebView` tag for the guest contents. What is more, we subscribed to the new-window event to force any request for opening a new window from the WebView to open in an external browser. Finally, we created a simple router to serve navigation in the feed menu.

Index

www.ingramcontent.com/pod-product-compliance
Lightning Source LLC
Chambersburg PA
CBHW060516060326
40690CB00017B/3298

* 9 7 8 1 7 8 8 2 9 5 6 9 7 *